THE OKLAHOMA POETS LAUREATE

A Sourcebook, History, and Anthology

MONGREL EMPIRE PRESS
NORMAN, OKLAHOMA, UNITED STATES OF AMERICA

2015

FIRST EDITION, 2015

The Oklahoma Poets Laureate
© 2014 by Shawn Holliday

ISBN 978-0-9903204-3-2

Cover Image
Some Oklahoma Poets Laureate
designed by Mongrel Empire Press

See image acknowledgments for photos.

MONGREL EMPIRE PRESS
NORMAN, OK

ONLINE CATALOGUE: WWW.MONGRELEMPIRE.ORG

This publisher is a proud member of

[clmp]

COUNCIL OF LITERARY MAGAZINES & PRESSES
w w w . c l m p . o r g

Book Design: Mongrel Empire Press using iWork Pages

THE OKLAHOMA POETS LAUREATE

A Sourcebook, History, and Anthology

Collected & Edited

by

Shawn Holliday, Ph.D.

PREFACE

In August 2009, I moved to Oklahoma from Kentucky, the state where I had been previously teaching college for ten years. Soon after arriving in Alva to chair the English, Foreign Language, and Humanities Department at Northwestern Oklahoma State University (NWOSU), I decided that I wanted to learn more about my new home state, so I began looking for literary works that were either set in Oklahoma or were written by Oklahoma authors. After conducting initial research, I was surprised to learn that no anthology of Oklahoma literature existed. Having been born in Kentucky and raised in West Virginia, I was used to living in Appalachia, a region with a strong literary tradition where university presses supported local literature. It was hard for me to believe that the University of Oklahoma Press had little interest in publishing fiction and poetry, especially since Oklahoma was one of the first states to establish and sponsor a poet laureate position. After starting on this book, however, I learned that an anthology of Oklahoma literature had been published on-line and was republished in print in 2010 as '*Ain't Nobody That Can Sing Like Me*': *New Oklahoma Writing*. This anthology, however, did not include previous 19th and 20th century Oklahoma poets and writers, whose work I was looking for. Unfortunately, Oklahoma's earliest authors had been largely forgotten.

This volume, then, is the result of my disbelief. Feeling the need to learn about the literature and history of my new home, I took it upon myself to research the lives and works of Oklahoma's twenty poets laureate, which would provide me with the foundation needed to understand the state and its people. Unfortunately for Oklahoma, it took an outsider to take on this project.

The intention of this anthology is to provide basic information about Oklahoma's poets laureate to lay-readers, students, and scholars alike. The book's introduction provides details about the position's ninety-two-year history followed by sections on each poet that include a brief biography, a bibliography of selected primary and secondary works, and a handful of representative poems. As an anthology, this book is in no way meant to be exhaustive. Hopefully, readers will be inspired to find out more about their favorite poets by doing their own reading and by conducting their own research. While the poet laureate position is currently alive and well in Oklahoma, its history and its early poets have been forgotten and neglected for far too long. Because it is difficult to find information on the early poets laureate, their work is emphasized over contemporary poets in this volume. I am optimistic, however, that this book will create a better appreciation for all of the poets' work in the minds of Oklahoma's citizens.

Of course, I could not have undertaken a project of this magnitude alone. I am appreciative of the following people, all of whom were helpful in getting this book into print after four years of hard work. I am especially indebted to the staff of NWOSU's J. W. Martin Library for help with preliminary research. Specific individuals include Susan Jeffries, Director of Libraries; Cindy Rich, former Research/Instructional Services Librarian; and Lisa Herning Zarrella, former Library Assistant. Pam Davidson, former Government Documents Technician and current Collection Services Assistant, was especially helpful in tracking down hard-to-find items via interlibrary loan. She was a joy to work with and was instrumental in locating many of the books and articles that I needed.

Also helpful were Ruth Ann Evans, Librarian at the Enid Public Library, who found newspaper articles on Bess Truitt, and my former student and research assistant, Debie Hyden, who found information on many of the early poets laureate.

I would also like to thank Angelia Case for helping to design promotional materials and for her support of this project, and Nathan Brown, Oklahoma's nineteenth poet laureate, who convinced me of the book's importance after I had given up on ever completing it.

Out of everyone, however, I am most indebted to Jeanetta Calhoun Mish, who immediately agreed to publish this volume just after hearing about it via email. Her enthusiasm encouraged me to finish after three years of failed attempts to find a publisher. Without her and Mongrel Empire Press, this book surely would not have seen the light of day.

Shawn Holliday, Ph.D.
Alva, OK, December 2013

For John Teel, Edmund Taft, Nancy Lang, and A. E. Stringer,
my mentors at Marshall University

Introduction

A BRIEF HISTORY OF THE OKLAHOMA
POET LAUREATE POSITION

While the original idea of the poet laureate came from ancient Greece, where the government presented a laurel wreath to a poet in recognition of especial achievement or talent, the concept made its way to twentieth-century America via seventeenth-century England when the practice of appointing a poet of the monarchy to write about royal births and deaths, military victories, and scientific achievements became an officially-recognized post upon its presentation to John Dryden in 1670.[1] Because the concept of the poet laureate was long associated in the United States with such English pomposities as "poets groveling before lords and trying to dress up hereditary idiots in velvet prosody," many Americans viewed the idea of a national poet as monarchical, unprofitable, sissified, and undemocratic.[2] Many poets also balked at the proposition, believing that occasional verse would cause more doggerel to be written than great poetry.[3] Subsequently, the United States was well over two hundred years old when Congress finally created the official post of "Poet Laureate Consultant in Poetry to the Library of Congress" in 1985.[4] Since Robert Penn Warren first accepted the national position in 1986, nineteen poets have served renewable eight month terms, carrying out the stated purpose of raising "the national consciousness to a greater appreciation of the reading and writing of poetry."[5] To carry out this goal, many of the U.S. poets laureate created their own initiatives to increase the public's awareness of verse. Robert Häss

1

started a national student competition; Joseph Brodsky made poetry available in such public spaces as airports, bus stations, and hotel rooms; and Billy Collins began the Poetry 180 initiative, which allowed high school students to read or hear a poem for every day of the school year.[6]

Although the United States was slow to embrace the idea of a national poet laureate, many state governments were much quicker in their acceptance. The first seventeen states to appoint poet laureates were from the American south and west, locations usually associated with political conservatism and cultural backwardness by the northeastern literary elite.[7] To defend against such stereotypes, many governments created this position to promote the idea that their states were civilized places that held unique cultural offerings.[8] Not only did this claim help to raise the self-esteem of state citizens, allowing them to take pride in home-grown traditions and values, but it also helped to promote tourism and industry in these isolated regions of the country, allowing armchair travelers to experience a place off the beaten path through the state poet's verse. Consequently, California became the first state to appoint a poet laureate in 1915. During the succeeding decade, nine other states quickly followed suit, including, in chronological order, Colorado, Nebraska, Oregon, Oklahoma, Idaho, Arkansas, Georgia, Kentucky, and West Virginia.[9] Hence, Oklahoma was the fifth state to appoint its own poet laureate.

On June 21, 1923, fifteen-and-one-half years after Oklahoma was admitted to the Union as the forty-sixth state, Governor Jack C. Walton named Violet McDougal as the state's first poet laureate. However, Walton's choice was not without controversy, as it was one of many instances of patronage (and other political problems) that plagued him during his ten months in office until his impeachment in November 1923.[10] While most poets laureate were appointed by governors for their depiction of the landscape and people of their home state, McDougal's poems rarely dealt with Oklahoma. In her only book, *Wandering Fires*, which she published with her sister Mary in 1925, only three of her thirty-six poems—"The War Drum," "The Oil Fire," and "The Phantom Round-up"—could be said to deal with Oklahoma directly. While McDougal indirectly references American Indians, the oil industry, and cowboy culture in her poetry, she never mentions the state by name.[11] In actuality, most of her verse depicted other places where she had lived, visited, or read about: New York, Florida, Kentucky, and the Bahamas.

It was not until later that the reason for McDougal's appointment became clear. Apparently, Walton created the position as a favor to the poet's mother, Myrtle Archer McDougal, who had been serving as a leading member of Oklahoma's Democratic Party for a decade.[12] In 1913 she was appointed as an Honorary Democratic Committeewoman, a post that became official in 1920. During this time, she began attending Democratic National Conventions and participating in party activities, all of which lent her political muscle in the state by the mid-1920s.[13] As biographer Marilyn Hoder-Salmon notes, "Myrtle never hesitated in using her influence to promote the ambitions of the talented McDougal daughters. One sees her touch in such events as the naming of Violet as Poet Laureate of Oklahoma and the appointment of Mary to a Washington post under Herbert Hoover."[14] Since Myrtle McDougal was instrumental in organizing some of Oklahoma's first literary societies, she found it only natural to use her influence to achieve state-wide recognition for Violet's poetry, even if it did not deal with Oklahoma directly.[15] Violet's lack of enthusiasm for the state, a place where she had rarely lived since becoming a teenager, led her to do little during her tenure to advance the appreciation of poetry by Oklahomans or to raise the cultural stock of the state within the nation.

This inauspicious start for Oklahoma's poets laureate would carry on well into the 1990s due to political favors given and impulsive decisions made on the part of the state's governors. As historians W. David Baird and Danney Goble note, "For decades Oklahomans and others had considered the state's political leadership less an assembly of statesmen than a cast of characters in an odd, never-ending public spectacle . . . Americans, both in and outside Oklahoma, had come to agree that this was a state generally long on screwball politics and short on responsible leadership."[16] As a result, Oklahoma's youthfulness and naïvete negatively affected the state's poets laureate; the governors' choices often illustrated just how foolish the state's politicians actually were.

Because disinterest in verse prevailed in Governor Walton's three direct successors, Oklahoma's next poet laureate was not named until eight years later when Paul Kroeger was appointed by Governor William H. D. "Alfalfa Bill" Murray in 1931. If Walton's appointment of McDougal was due to nepotism, Murray's appointment of Kroeger was due to whimsy since his decision was based on having received one of Kroeger's poems in the mail, a choice indicative of the governor's uneducated, headstrong nature.[17] Unknowledgeable of whether Kroeger was prolific or if his verse held any value, Murray soon named him to the position despite Kroeger's acknowledgement that "I am no poet, only a dreamer of dreams."[18] Since Kroeger's interests also included music, religion, and furniture restoration, his poetic output was slight, his quality varied, and his themes were more universal than regional.[19] Like McDougal, his verse rarely depicted his home state. Although he is notable for being the only male of the first six poets laureate and also the youngest poet ever to receive the honor, his tenure was unremarkable since his poetry was never collected in a book and because he often published under the nom de plume David Nash, weakening his presence as one who could influence social or literary change.[20]

Almost ten years elapsed until the state's third poet laureate was commissioned. This occurred in 1940, when Acting Governor James E. Berry selected Jennie Harris Oliver, the first writer truly deserving of the tribute. While the poet laureate position had floundered for almost twenty years in the hands of younger poets who failed to define its duties and responsibilities adequately, Oliver provided an appropriate template since she had been serving as the state's unofficial literary ambassador for years. It also helped that that the Poetry Society of Oklahoma, of which Oliver was a member, had been organized in the meantime, helping to provide support for the state's poets and direction for its governors. Both before and during her appointment, Oliver mentored younger writers, attended women's club meetings, and read from her work all over the state.[21] Her verse was also the first to depict "nature as it existed in Oklahoma—the red earth and white dunes, the hills and valleys, the ferns and flowers," all of which revealed her "fondness for Oklahoma's red land.[22] A good example of Oliver's love for Oklahoma appears in the poem "'Here' (Oklahoma)":

> Here are no stern deep snows and frozen rivers;
> Here are few long, gray rains. We have the sun—
> A summer so replete there is no telling
> When it is done.

Here we have winter as a white face, smiling
And after it, the warm rain vanishing.
A night of wind, a day of wild bird singing,
And flowers spring.

We have the mountains, not too deep for climbing;
And we have the canyons, not too deep to cross,
What we have planted, gods or man may harvest—
There is no loss.

And here the stars are very low, and friendly;
The moon is whiter than the one we knew.
If earth and streams are red, we have the skyline,
And it is blue.

Here is the soul of all that Nature promised;
New friends to know! new books to read and lend.
If snow was mother, then the Sun is stepland—
A journey's end.[23]

Because Oliver's stories and poems were known both nationally and internationally and because of her dedication to advancing literature in Oklahoma, Jennie Harris Oliver stands as the model for all later poets laureate by becoming an integral state resource. Her celebration of the state's landscape and people also provided an appropriate model for those who followed. Unfortunately, many of her successors ignored her precedent, being unwilling or unable to consider the post as more than a ceremonial one.

When Jennie Harris Oliver's tenure as Oklahoma's poet laureate ended with her death on June 3, 1942, the state took several months to grieve until Governor Robert S. Kerr selected Della Iona Cann Young as her replacement.[24] Although his first appointment was a misstep since Young was known more as an educator and folklorist than as a poet, Kerr's two subsequent choices showed that he was the first governor who truly understood the complexities of the position. Realizing that he had the power to recognize many talented poets during his time in office by granting one-year terms, Kerr next selected formalist Anne Ruth Semple in 1944, the first American Indian woman of the early poets laureate and the most linguistically sophisticated. In her only published book, *Prairie-Born* (1942), Semple employed a wide array of classical forms from aphorisms and epigrams to villanelles and narratives in blank verse. Like Jennie Harris Oliver before her, Semple's verse is grounded in Oklahoma's landscape, which she celebrates by turning midwestern folklore, myth, and witticisms into verse. Consequently, most of her poems depict "the vastness, the fertility, and the enthralling beauty of the prairies" through the lens of her dual Scottish and Choctaw heritages.[25]

After Semple's term expired in 1945, Kerr next appointed Bess Truitt, who had participated as a child in the Cherokee Outlet Land Run of 1893. Although her poems were not as complex and varied as Semple's, Truitt's verse was similar in that it expressed a love for the state's people and landscape. Her only published book of poetry, *Thistle Down and Prairie Rose* (1940), contained short, imagistic poems about the state's flora and longer narrative poems about Oklahoma's land runs, the latter of which remained a preoccupation for her throughout her life. A typical example of Truitt's work is "In Fee," which employs a first person narrator in the voice of a settler who takes comfort in the memories he has of the 160 acres he now must sell:

> I sold the hundred and sixty,
> Delivered the deed today;
> But nothing was said of the wood thrush-song,
>> Or the light that softly lay
>> On the rim of the open prairie,
>> Or the fragrance of new-moan hay.
>
> It did not include transfer
> Of the wind's low symphony
> Idly swinging the nests of birds,
> That hang in each maple tree
> Or the title to love and service.
> All these, I hold in fee.[26]

Although this poem is uncharacteristic of Truitt's verse in that it is an elegy, it does represent the in-depth knowledge the poet had of the people and places which she depicted in both good and bad times. As Truitt's poetry suggests, her main activity as poet laureate was to help preserve the history of the Cherokee Outlet and of the Chisholm Trail, public service work that she had undertaken well before her appointment. To support her efforts, she held memberships in such organizations as the Oklahoma Poetry Society, the Oklahoma Historical Society, and the National League of American Pen Women.²⁷ She also edited the *Journal of the Sons and Daughters of the Cherokee Strip* for ten years and coedited the regional literary journal *Red Earth*, named in honor of Jennie Harris Oliver's poem and book of the same name, for four years. Because of her long devotion to northwestern Oklahoma's literature and history, she was named to the Oklahoma Hall of Fame in 1959. A poetry society, The Truitteers, was later founded in her honor.²⁸

Although Bess Truitt's appointment was set to expire in 1946, Governor Kerr did not appoint a seventh poet laureate. His four successors failed to do so as well. Consequently, the momentum that had started during his one term in office stopped until May 1963 when Governor Henry Bellmon commissioned Delbert Davis. At this time, Bellmon also created the position of poet laureate emeritus for Bess Truitt, who many considered to be the state's poet laureate in the seventeen-year interim even though her tenure was to last only one year.²⁹ Truitt held this emeritus position for almost ten years, ending with her death in 1972.

While 1963 should seem historically modern in the minds of contemporary readers, Governor Bellmon's choice of Delbert Davis was a step backward for the Oklahoma poet laureate position, one that would have been more appropriate had it occurred during the 1920s or 1930s. Appointed at the age of 80, Davis's folk poetry had much more in common with the hardships of pioneer farmers and the economic difficulties of Depression-era families than with Cold War angst and space age rhetoric. For the most part, Davis's verse deals with sentimental themes written in a western dialect that presents literal rather than figurative or associative meanings. He was unable to elevate everyday objects to poetic importance, undercutting his subject matter by hard, end-stopped rhymes most associated with children's verse. For example, in "Whittling Sticks," Davis provides no poetic tension other than the obvious, relying on the change of season to resolve the poem: "Whittling sticks for passtime / Thinking of home, yum, yum, / Pacing the depot platform / Wishing the train would come [. . . .] From June to late November / We argue Con and Pro / all things till bleak December / Adjourns us with its snow."³⁰

Unfortunately, Davis's selection as poet laureate continued the tradition of choosing "white haired ladies and delicate literary men" who wrote nostalgically about the state with no intention of confronting major issues of the day.³¹ While Oklahoma's poets laureate have generally been "fairly representative of the state's population and culture" in regards to sex and geographic location, the choices made during the 1960s and 1970s remained problematic since Oklahoma's governors seemed unwilling to define the position adequately.[32] Because of this, it remained a post determined more by individual whims and pleasures than by careful consideration. The governors' ignorance of literature in general (and of poetry especially) caused many to rely on recommendations given by the state's literary societies, which often made selections based on nepotism rather than worth. This problem plagued the position from the beginning. Unfortunately, the quality of the poets laureate remained uneven because their relevance to the issues and mores of the period changed from appointment to appointment. This became especially problematic when racial, sexual, and political upheavals began changing the national culture.

While Davis's verse was often sophomoric, depicting a bygone era with uncomplicated rhyme schemes, his successor in 1966, Rudolph N. Hill, explored more sophisticated themes that were undercut as well by monotonous hard rhymes and end-stopped lines, mirroring the doggerel about which many national poets had warned. However, by the time of his appointment, Hill's poetry had been appearing in regional and national periodicals for more than fifty years, which did make him worthy of the state's attention.[33] By the end of his term he had published seven books of poetry by small regional presses, the titles of which—*Whipping-Tree* and *Wagon Trails Farewell*; *America Forever* (1942), *Star of Peace on Trail of Cibola* (1954), and *From Country Lanes to Space Age Dawn* (1968)—illustrate their pertinence to contemporary events and 1960s culture. Clearly, Hill's background in journalism and experiences as a lawyer and judge, which prompted his politically-motivated appointment to the poet laureate position, kept him engaged with issues in ways that his predecessors were not even if his verse was plagued by traditional forms that had grown passé by the 1960s.

Out of respect for Hill, Governor Dewey Bartlett named him as Oklahoma's second poet laureate emeritus upon replacing him with Leslie A. McRill in 1970.[34] While McRill was like Hill in exploring themes that were influenced by his scholarly work, his age at the time of appointment, eighty-four, made him the oldest person ever named to the position.[35] Although he, too, used traditional verse forms that undercut his complex subjects—especially troubling was his use of

European forms to depict American Indian history and myth—he remained mentally engaged with such contemporary issues as the Civil Rights Movement, the Vietnam War, and computerized dating despite his inability to do much with the position physically. While much of his verse also was like Hill's in valorizing the state by "affirming traditional values of family, community, and religion," McRill left Oklahoma in 1974 to settle in Cincinnati, Ohio, where he spent the last eight years of his life.[36] Despite this fact, he remained Oklahoma's poet laureate for three years in absentia.

Although Maggie Culver Fry was also elderly at the time of her appointment by Governor David Boren in 1977, her verse was more universal than regional in subject matter, which lent her a larger reading audience than many of her forerunners. While Fry often wrote elegiac love poems as well as verse that explored American Indian themes, she also was interested in higher existential questions that expressed themselves through religious and metaphysical musings. A good example is her poem "Eternal," where she ties herself to all of humanity through her deep connection with ancestry and time:

> The umbilical cord
> Of my basic beginning,
> Still draws me back
> To the source of the river;
> Where life from the loom
> Keeps spinning and spinning . . .
> No hand can undo
> And no power can sever . . .
> I am bound, I am bound . . .
> To Forever, forever.[37]

That Fry was able to make such universal connections in her verse makes her one of the least provincial of the state's poets laureate. By the time of her appointment, her reputation was already well established through her frequent publishing of nonfiction in *Oklahoma Today* and other regional magazines. Although her work received much national acclaim—her second book, *The Umbilical Cord* (1971) was nominated for a Pulitzer Prize—the poet laureate position was unfortunately ignored by Oklahoma's governors for almost two decades during her tenure.[38] Like Bess Truitt earlier, Maggie Culver Fry held the post for eighteen years, well into the mid-1990s.[39] While her split Anglo and Cherokee heritage continued to lend her work relevance because of the literary community's growing interest in multiculturalism, her age did not allow her to do much with the post physically during the last years of her tenure. Even though she mentored younger poets, held public readings, and visited schools early on, her age later forced her to treat the title as more ceremonial than participatory, a circumstance that had positive consequences starting with her replacement.

Having been plagued for over fifty years with one-term governors who could not establish political continuity within the state due to a one-term mandate in the Oklahoma Constitution, Oklahoma's poet laureate position seemed doomed to a certain death during the 1970s and 1980s after a string of elderly poets made the post seem culturally irrelevant. Oklahoma could well have done away with the position for lack of interest by the government and its citizens. For the most part, the ten poets who held the position since 1923 tried to cobble together a state literary tradition without the support of a university press, in many cases publishing their own work and supporting each other's efforts in the face of a largely disinterested public. Unlike poets in other regions of the country, Appalachia and the south, Oklahoma did not have a strong tradition of storytelling or poetry that was continuously celebrated. The survival of the position called for a strong governor who held an interest in the arts and a vision for the post, one who would make the state poet laureate relevant to a modern Oklahoma and an honorary fixture in the state's government. David Walters, who served as governor from 1991–95, proved to be this leader. Although Walters was prodded by a legislator from Oklahoma City who endorsed a constituent's self-interested plea to appoint a laureate every two years, the governor also yearned to make the laureate post culturally important, calling on the poet laureate for active duty and participation within the state.

Although Governor Walters did not run for a second term due to being embroiled in an election violation scandal, his dedication to renewing Oklahoma's poet laureate position fit with his commitment to increasing funding for education and his interest in the arts.[40] In 1994, during his last year in office, he supported legislation that helped to define the purpose and parameters of the post, making regular appointments a part of the governor's duties. The full text of Oklahoma's law 25–98.4 that he endorsed states:

> There is hereby designated the honorary position of State
> Poet Laureate.

> The State Poet Laureate shall be appointed by the Governor from lists provided by poetry societies and organizations and such person shall have this honorary position for a period of two (2) years. Each appointment shall be made by January 1 of every odd year beginning January 1, 1995. The person appointed to the honorary position of State Poet Laureate shall not be considered a state official or a state employee for such person's service in the honorary position of State Poet Laureate. The State PoetLaureate shall not be prohibited because of said appointed position from:
>
> Running for and being elected to any office in the state or a political subdivision of the state; or
>
> Being employed as a classified or unclassified employee of the state or a political subdivision of the state.[41]

Unlike the previous seventy-two years, Oklahoma now would have a poet laureate appointed consistently. Because the law made no provision for term limits, poets could possibly serve more than one term if their commitment to the position was found worthy of an additional commission. So far, this has occurred only once when Francine Ringold was renewed for a second term from 2005 to 2007.

Although a few missteps have occurred since the law was added in 1994, Oklahoma's recent governors have done a good job of appointing qualified persons to the poet laureate position. For the most part, the poets of the modern era are much less provincial than their forebears, writing complex verse on a wide range of confessional topics and themes. Most have found the position more relevant than ever, helping to calm the public's fears by contemplating the ramifications of the terrorist bombing of the A. P. Murrah Building in Oklahoma City on April 19, 1995, a scar on the Oklahoma psyche that may never heal. Because the Oklahoma Humanities Council coordinates nominations from the state's cultural organizations on behalf of the governor and helps to schedule readings for appointees, it provides quality control to ensure that only the most qualified individuals are recommended; those who will promote poetry statewide and who will commit to community outreach efforts.[42] While such names as Betty Shipley, Joe Kreger, and Carl Sennhenn may be known only to Oklahoma's literary community, others like Carol Hamilton and Jim Barnes have important regional reputations while Francine Ringold and N. Scott Momaday are well-known nationally and internationally. Ringold's service from 2003 to 2007 and Momaday's from 2007 to 2009 illustrate that Oklahoma's poet laureate position has matured enough to honor the state's poets by helping them to promote the literary arts for the good of Oklahoma's citizenry. These poets, along with Jim Barnes, are also the first to hold doctorate of philosophy degrees, which illustrates the state's growing cultural sophistication and openness toward academic thinking at the start of the new millennium.

Ringold's work as the editor of *Nimrod: The International Journal of Prose and Poetry* and her dedication to teaching the physically challenged and the elderly show that the state's poet laureate can do much more than just advance poetry.[43] Similarly, Pulitzer Prize winner N. Scott Momaday has helped to raise Oklahoma's literary stock by bringing American Indian issues to national attention and for having taught at such prestigious institutions as the University of California, Berkeley; Stanford University; and the University of Arizona.[44] Momaday's Kiowa and Cherokee ancestry helps him to de-centralize the importance of whiteness in the growing global culture by depicting American Indian traditions that replace dominant Anglo myths with older yet subordinate ones. His book *The Way to Rainy Mountain* (1976) is especially important in this process. For the most part, he is interested in translating "oral traditions into literary ones" to prod his readers into understanding their intricate relationship to family, history, environment, and mother earth.[45] Unlike his predecessors Rudolph Hill and Leslie McRill, Momaday does not rely upon European forms to depict his Native American themes. In 2007, President George W. Bush presented Momaday with the National Medal of Arts "for his writings and his work that celebrate and preserve Native American art and tradition," illustrating his importance to America's national culture.[46]

While Momaday's successor, Jim Barnes, was also a fine choice for his regional reputation, his replacement, Eddie Wilcoxen, was problematic since he is mainly known as a martial arts instructor who privately publishes his own work. However, Wilcoxen's radio show on KWHW in Altus did ensure that Oklahomans would be exposed to poetry through broadcasting as well.[47] Only time will tell if the state's future governors will continue to sustain the position with poets of both literary and social merit.

Today, forty-two states have poet laureates. Although their purpose and influence may differ slightly, each promotes the literary arts within their state while also celebrating the landscape, people, history, and culture from whence they came. Like many of these, Oklahoma's poet laureate position is currently alive and well, creating a better appreciation for the arts among Oklahomans and bringing much-needed attention to the peoples and subcultures that make up the Union's forty-sixth state.

Fortunately, Oklahoma's nineteenth poet laureate, Nathan Brown, returned high quality poetry to the position. Even though he holds a doctorate of philosophy from the University of Oklahoma, his verse is easily accessible to the average reader, which made him a perfect candidate for the position.[48] Within the first months of his appointment, he gave readings at a number of the state's college campuses and literary societies, fulfilling his view of the appointment as making him a literary "Johnny Appleseed," whose duty it is to "spread the word on contemporary poetry and Oklahoma's traditions."[49] This and Brown's interests in music and photography (as well as his relatively young age of forty-eight) ensured that his term was more participatory than ceremonial.

A typical example of Brown's verse can be found in the poem "Lowland Heretic," in which he uses humor and self-deprecation to depict the political divide that currently separates the country. Here, Brown presents his speaker as a snake alienated from the state's largest political party, whose conservative members view him as a threat, one who is opposed to both their religious beliefs and traditional way of life:

> Down by the base of a wheat stalk
> in the well-tended fields of Lower-
> Great-Plains-Republicans, I lie . . .
>
> a brown slithering Democrat,
> narrowly escaping the occasional blaze
> of buckshot and boot soles at cockfights,
> roosters with razor blades.
>
> [. . .]
>
> I now raise
> a sinful hand up and out toward
> the softly shaking head of St. Jude
> in hopes he'll rescue this lonely lost cause
> from the rage of a red-faced denomination

that lords an iron-fist domination
over the souls of good people [. . .][50]

Such political overtness is rare in a poet laureate. This poem, in its depiction of the snake needing saving from the people, speaks to the importance of dissenting voices who offer alternate views on life and the arts within the state. That Governor Fallin saw fit to appoint Brown speaks to the open-mindedness of the Oklahoma's representatives who are bringing qualified poets to the position.

On November 24, 2014, Fallin, who had just been reelected to a second term, named Benjamin Myers as the state's twentieth poet laureate. Like Brown, he is a Ph.D. who writes accessible verse. Readers can relate to the contemporary issues and religious themes that he explores in his two books: *Elegy for Trains* (2010) and *Lapse Americana* (2013). Like his immediate predecessors, Myers will be asked to make six appearances for free events that the Oklahoma Humanities Council will help coordinate. As always, however, there will be no expectation for him to "compose official poems or to recite for state occasions."[51] When asked if he had a particular platform to promote with the position, Myers said that wanted not only to promote poetry by other, lesser-known Oklahoma poets but also to work with children and high school students to encourage them to read and write poetry throughout their lives.[52]

When Benjamin Myers' tenure expires on December 31, 2016, it will be exciting to see what Oklahoman will take his place and what platform he or she will use to promote poetry. Hopefully, that poet will continue the recent trend of communicating the greatness of Oklahoma and its people within the state and to the rest of the nation. Recent appointments have shown that that Oklahoma's governors are now interested in promoting the best verse that the state has to offer, imaginative in style and progressive in content. Because of this, the future for poetry is bright within the state.

A Timeline of the Oklahoma Poet Laureate Position

Year	Laureate	Location	Governor
1923	Violet McDougal	Sapulpa	Jack C. Walton
1931	Paul Kroeger	Guthrie	William H. D. Murray
1940	Jenny Harris Oliver	Fallis	James E. Berry (acting)
1943	Della Iona Cann Young	Cheyenne	Robert S. Kerr
1944	Anne Ruth Semple	Caddo	Robert S. Kerr
1945	Bess Truitt	Enid	Robert S. Kerr
1963	Delbert Davis	Wellston	Henry L. Bellmon
1966	Rudolph N. Hill	Wewoka	Henry L. Bellmon
1970	Leslie A. McRill	Oklahoma City	Dewey F. Bartlett
1977	Maggie Culver Fry	Claremore	David L. Boren
1995	Carol Hamilton	Midwest City	Francis A. Keating
1997	Betty Shipley	Edmond	Francis A. Keating

Year	Laureate	Location	Governor
1998	Joe Kreger	Tonkawa	Francis A. Keating
2001	Carl Sennhenn	Norman	Francis A. Keating
2003	Francine Ringold	Tulsa	Brad Henry
2007	N. Scott Momaday	Lawton	Brad Henry
2009	Jim Barnes	Summerfield	Brad Henry
2011	Eddie Wilcoxen	Altus	Brad Henry
2013	Nathan Brown	Norman	Mary Fallin
2015	Benjamin Myers	Chandler	Mary Fallin

Notes

*This essay first appeared, in slightly different form, in the *Chronicles of Oklahoma* 91, no. 2 (Summer 2013): 172–91.

¹*Encyclopedia of Oklahoma History and Culture*, s.v. "Poets Laureate," by Patricia Yarbrough, accessed March 24, 2013, http://digital.library.okstate.edu/encyclopedia/entries/P/PO002.html; Kate Pickert, "A Brief History of the Poet Laureate," *Time*, July 24, 2008, http://www.time.com/time/magazine/article/0,9171,1826277,00.html. Even though the position of poet laureate did not become an official government post in England until 1670, King James I began the regular practice of appointing a poet to the monarchy when he granted the honor to Ben Jonson in 1617. However, many English monarchs before King James maintained favored poets at court, including Geoffrey Chaucer for Richard II, William the Pilgrim for Richard-the-Lion-Hearted, and John Skelton for Henry VII.

²Lance Morrow, "Time Essay: America Needs a Poet Laureate, Maybe," *Time*, August 25, 1980, http://www.time.com/time/magazine/article/0,9171,949020.html.

³Ibid.

⁴Although the official position of "Poet Laureate Consultant in Poetry to the Library of Congress" was not authorized until 1985, many poets served as a "Consultant in Poetry to the Library of Congress" from 1937 to 1986, a position that held a similar function as the current national poet laureate without the title. These writers, including such names as Allen Tate, William Carlos Williams, Robert Lowell, and Gwendolyn Brooks, were sometimes considered the nation's unofficial poets laureate. Often, the favorite poets of presidents were also considered unofficial poets laureate since they spoke at inaugurations or visited the White House. These include Robert Frost for John F. Kennedy, James Dickey for Jimmy Carter, Maya Angelou for Bill Clinton, and Elizabeth Alexander for Barack Obama.

⁵"About the Position of Poet Laureate Consultant in Poetry," Library of Congress, accessed March 24, 2013, http://www.loc.gov/poetry/about_laureate.html.

⁶Pickert, "A Brief History"; "About the Position"; Billy Collins, "Poetry 180: A Poem a Day in American High Schools," Library of Congress, accessed March 24, 2013,
http://www.loc.gov/poetry/180/.

⁷Roger Penn Cuff, "An Appraisal of the American Poets Laureate," *Peabody Journal of Education* 25, no.4 (1948): 157-62, 164-66.

[8]Yarbrough, "Poets Laureate."

[9]Cuff, "An Appraisal," 157; Peter Armenti, "U.S. State Poets Laureate," Main Reading Room, Library of Congress, accessed March 24, 2013, http://www.loc.gov/rr/main/poets/.

[10]David W. Baird and Danney Goble, *Oklahoma: A History* (Norman: University of Oklahoma Press, 2008), 186. Among the many indiscretions committed by Governor Walton included making a large number of political appointments for his friends and political supporters; declaring martial law in Tulsa during his fight to clean up the Ku Klux Klan (a popular organization that had many members in the state legislature at the time); using troops to block the meeting of a grand jury convened to investigate his misdeeds; and threatening to parole prisoners in retaliation for his impeachment hearings undertaken in the Oklahoma House of Representatives.

[11]Mary McDougal and Violet McDougal, *Wandering Fires: Poems* (Boston: Stratford, 1925), 3-5, 50-51, 58-59.

[12]Marilyn Hoder-Salmon, "Leader of Oklahoma's 'Timid Sisters,'" *Chronicles of Oklahoma* 60, no. 3 (Fall 1982): 332.

[13]Ibid., 338-39.

[14]Ibid., 341.

[15]Ibid., 340.

[16]Baird and Goble, *Oklahoma: A History*, 237.

[17]"Pleases Governor; New Poet Laureate," *Gettysburg (PA) Times*, September 15, 1931; Baird and Goble, *Oklahoma: A History*, 226-27.

[18]Mary Hays Marable and Elaine Boylan, *A Handbook of Oklahoma Writers* (Norman: University of Oklahoma Press, 1939), 66-67.

[19]Lyle H. Boren and Dale Boren, *Who is Who in Oklahoma* (Guthrie, OK: Co-operative, 1935), 280-81.

[20]Marable and Boylan, *A Handbook*, 66.

[21]Bess Truitt, "Jennie Harris Oliver," *Chronicles of Oklahoma* 22, no. 2 (Summer 1944): 138-42.

[22]Cuff, "An Appraisal," 161.

[23]Jennie Harris Oliver, *Red Earth* (Kansas City, MO: Burton, 1937), 39.

[24]*Encyclopedia of Oklahoma History and* Culture, s.v. "Oliver, Jennie Harris (1864-1942)," by Linda D. Wilson, accessed March 30, 2013, http://digital.library.okstate.edu/encyclopedia/entries/O/OL003.html.

[25]Cuff, "An Appraisal" 162.

[26]Bess Truitt, *Thistle Down and Prairie Rose* (Kansas City, MO: Burton, 1940), 18.

[27]Wanda Pyle, "Who's Who Lists Three Enid Women," *Enid (OK) Morning News*, January 16, 1959.

[28]"Poet Laureate Emeritus Bessie Truitt Dies," *Enid Morning News*, August 21, 1972.

[29]"Bess Truitt's Poems Entered in Journal," *Enid Morning News*, May 25, 1963.

[30] Delbert Davis, *Pipe Dreams* (Guthrie, OK: Calkins, 1952), 33.

[31]Yarbrough, "Poets Laureate." Appointing poets who do not challenge the policies of state and national officials has been a tradition by governors across the country for the past century. Most recently, New Jersey Governor Jim McGreevey attempted to dismiss Imamu Amiri Baraka as the state's second poet laureate for reading his poem "Somebody Blew Up America" at the Geraldine R. Dodge Poetry Festival in September 2002, just one year after terrorist attacks on September 11, 2001. Baraka, however, refused to step down. Consequently, on October 17, 2002, a bill was introduced to abolish that state's poet laureate position; it passed and became law in July 2003, thus ending the short-lived position in New Jersey.

[32]Ibid. To date, none of Oklahoma's twenty poets laureate have been of African American descent, although this racial group currently makes up almost 10 percent of the state's population.

[33]Marable and Boylan, *A Handbook*, 61-63.

[34]Hill maintained his appointment as poet laureate emeritus until 1977 when Leslie A. McRill was given the position after being replaced as poet laureate by Maggie Culver Fry.

[35]Yarbrough, "Poets Laureate."

[36]Ibid.

[37]Maggie Culver Fry, *The Umbilical Cord* (Muskogee, OK: Oklahoma Printing, 1971), 2.

[38]Veima Neiberding, "Maggie Culver Fry, Cherokee," Western History Collections, University of Oklahoma, May 15, 1971, http://digital.libraries.ou.edu/whc/duke/transcripts/T-654-2.pdf.

[39]Yarbrough, "Poets Laureate."

[40]"Oklahoma Governors Since Statehood," accessed April 6, 2013, http://www.ok.gov/governor/govlist.htm.

[41]"Oklahoma—State Poet Laureate," Main Reading Room, Library of Congress, accessed April 6, 2013, http://www.loc.gov/rr/main/poets/oklahoma.html.

[42]"State Poet Laureate," Oklahoma Humanities Council, accessed April 7, 2013, http://www.okhumanities.org/state-poet-laureate.

[43]Joe Myers, "Dr. Francine Ringold/Oklahoma Poet Laureate," Oklahoma Center for Poets and Writers, accessed April 7, 2013, <http://poetsandwriters.okstate.edu/OKauthor/ringold.html>.

[44]Anton Treuer, et al., "N. Scott Momaday," *Indian Nations of North America* (Washington, D.C.: National Geographic, 2010), 172.

[45]Howard Meredith, "N. Scott Momaday: A Man of Words," *World Literature Today: A Literary Quarterly of the University of Oklahoma* 64, no. 3 (1990): 405-07, <http://search.ebscohost.com/login.aspx?direct=true&db=mzh&AN=1990055751&site=ehost-live>.

[46]Truer et al., "N. Scott Momaday."

[47]"Eddie Wilcoxen," Oklahoma Humanities Council, accessed April 7, 2013, http://www.okhumanities.org/eddie-wilcoxen.

[48]"State Poet Laureate." Oklahoma Humanities Council

[49]Nathan Brown, interview with the author, April 22, 2013, Alva, OK.

[50]Nathan Brown, *Karma Crises: New and Selected Poems* (Norman, OK: Mescalita, 2012), 61.

[51]Ibid.

[52]Benjamin Myers, telephone interview with the author, December 2, 2014.

1923-1931

VIOLET MCDOUGAL

Violet Audrey McDougal, Oklahoma's first poet laureate, was born in Selmer, Tennessee, on December 19, 1893, to Donald A. McDougal, an attorney, and Myrtle Archer McDougal, a political activist who would later play major roles in the suffrage, world peace, and prohibition movements. Like her elder sisters Jennie and Mary, Violet spent her childhood in Tennessee until she moved with her parents in June 1904 to the railroad town of Sapulpa in Indian Territory, where her father had earlier "made the run" during the opening of the Cherokee Outlet. Here, the McDougals lived in a small cottage on South Elm Street, surrounded in town by Creek and Euchee Indians, farmers, cowboys, and oil men. Although Violet's mother often felt homesick for the south, forming women's groups to combat her increasing sense of loneliness and isolation, she saw Oklahoma as being tolerant of her political initiatives and decided to stay. Subsequently, she infused the women of the region and her three daughters with ideas about expanding the role of women in American society.

The McDougals lived modestly in Sapulpa for the next four years until Donald was given forty acres of land by an Indian family as payment for legal services rendered in getting their name added to Creek Tribal rolls. On a hunch, he had a well dug there and hit oil. With this stroke of luck, the McDougals became millionaires, one of the wealthiest families in town. They began enjoying their new-found wealth by purchasing a car, a luxury item at the time, and an impressive two-story house built in the Queen Anne style. To foster their daughters' love of the arts, they also bought a piano for their home and supported their attempts to write literature, an hereditary trait they received from their maternal grandmother, who had been an essayist; their maternal great aunts, who had dabbled in poetry and journalism; and their mother, who had written short stories and articles for newspapers.

The McDougal parents also used their money to ensure that their daughters received a good education by sending them to boarding schools outside of Oklahoma. Subsequently, Violet spent most of her teenage years in Texas and Colorado. For college, however, she returned home to attend the University of Oklahoma, where she made the decision to devote her time to poetry. While here, she became a member of Kappa Alpha Theta, the first Greek letter society for women that was organized with principles similar to those of men's fraternities. This would not be the last time that her mother's feminist influence and organizational skills would positively affect Violet's life.

After also attending the University of Missouri and Columbia University, Violet, like her sister Mary, focused on developing her poetic craft, spending much of her mid-to-late-twenties publishing poems in such periodicals as *The New York Times*, *The Daily Oklahoman*, *The San Antonio Express*, *The Argosy*, and *Literary Digest*. During the summer of 1923, she traveled to Georgetown, Connecticut, to write and collect poems for a book with her sister Mary. While here, she learned of her appointment on June 21st as Oklahoma's first poet laureate by Governor Jack C. Walton. Completely surprised by the news, Violet commented that "I have never seen Governor Walton in my life [. . .] I do not know why he gave me this appointment, unless it was at the suggestion of friends of mine. I don't know whether or not he ever read a poem of mine." Unknown at the time, she had received the honor from recommendations given by the Oklahoma Writer's Guild, the Poetry Guild of Norman, and various women's clubs in the state, all of which were either organized or heavily influenced by the poet's mother, Myrtle. Although Violet's appointment as the state's first poet laureate appeared to stem from nepotism (especially since her poems rarely dealt with Oklahoma), that did not stop her from becoming a human interest story in newspapers across the country, making her a minor celebrity during the mid-1920s.

This new-found notoriety lent a reading audience to Violet and Mary's book *Wandering Fires*. Published in 1925 by The Stratford Company, a Boston press, the volume collected 79 lyrics by the McDougal family: 36 by Violet, 42 by Mary, and 1 by Myrtle. Situated first in the volume, Violet's self-described landscape poems about the "new west"—missing such "old west" subjects as Indians, farmers, and pioneers—contrasted directly with Mary's more personal verse. Although Violet's poems relied heavily upon the rhyming conventions of formalist 19th Century poetry, they were distinctly modern in their exploration of new, casual subject matters: the thoughts of a vaudeville knife-thrower, the superstitions of fishermen, and the description of an oil fire. This tension between old and new also appeared as a theme in such poems as "The War Drum," "Jazz," and "Heredity," where the poet compared civilization to barbarism, exploring the limitations and dread of both. Such deft handling of diverse subject matters in a humorous way caused a reviewer for the *Oakland Tribune* to call the sisters "singers who sing of today and who do it with a fine zest and clear voice. They are not blind to the softer tones and not scornful of the carnival colors." This was especially true of Violet's poems, which were set in such wide-ranging places as Florida, Kentucky, Manhattan, and Sing-Sing prison.

After her tenure as Oklahoma's poet laureate expired in 1931, Violet continued writing poems and articles on poetry but failed to achieve the same level of success that had occurred during the 1920s. Her method of writing poems spontaneously based upon her mood— she wrote one on a piece of scrap paper while leaning on a door jamb and another on the back of a folding fan—caused her output to be erratic and intermittent. Although Violet edited *Flamingo Magazine* during the 1950s, she never again published a book of verse. She lived out her golden years in southern Florida close to her sister Mary, where their parents had earlier bought a vacation home and set up an oil business. Having dedicated much of her life to writing and literature, Violet McDougal never saw the need to marry, once commenting to the *Hoboken New Jersey Observer* that "you cannot be a real artist and marry [. . .] I think a girl must choose between marriage and an artistic career because if a girl marries that takes up so much of her life there is little time for anything else." She passed away in Coral Gables, Florida on April 28, 1989, at age 95. Her papers are housed at the University of Miami with her sister Mary's.

Selected Bibliography

Primary Works
McDougal, Mary, and Violet McDougal. *Wandering Fires: Poems.* Boston: Stratford, 1925.
McDougal, Violet. "Sea Devils." *San Antonio Express*, December 18, 1924. 12.

Secondary Works
"Girl Poet Laureate of Oklahoma Here." *New York Times*, July 5, 1923. Accessed 18 December 2013. <http://select.nytimes.com/gst/abstract.html?res=F7081FFA3B5417738DDDAC0894DF405B838EF1D3&scp=violet+mcdougal&st=p>.
Goins, Charles Robert, and Danney Goble. *Historical Atlas of Oklahoma.* 4th edition. Norman, OK: University of Oklahoma Press, 2006.
Hoder-Salmon, Marilyn. "Myrtle Archer McDougal: Leader of Oklahoma's 'Timid Sisters.'"
Chronicles of Oklahoma 60, no. 3 (1982): 332–43.
"Mary McDougal Axelson Papers (University of Miami)," <http://everglades.fiu.edu/reclaim/ collections/axelson.html>.
"McDougal, Violet, Author." *Who is Who in Oklahoma*. Eds. Lyle H. Boren and Dale Boren. Guthrie, OK: Co-operative, 1935. 361–62.
Moriarty, Edith. "With the Women of Today." *Middletown (NY) Daily Herald*, July 20, 1923. 11.
"Oklahoma's Poet Laureate Now Living in Georgetown." *Bridgeport (CT) Telegram*, Oct. 8, 1923. 4.
"Review of Wandering Fires: Poems, by Mary and Violet McDougal." *Oakland (CA) Tribune*, Aug. 2, 1925. 63.
"Violet McDougal." A *Handbook of Oklahoma Writers*. Eds. Mary Hays Marable and Elaine Boylan. Norman, OK: University of Oklahoma Press, 1939. 73.

Selected Poems by Violet McDougal

The Phantom Round-Up

Where the city sleeps in silence,
On a soft star-silvered night
There's a soundless phantom round-up once a year,
And the city seems to vanish
In a flood of ghostly light
While the streets and shops and buildings disappear.

Then a horde of phantom riders
Spur across the starlit waste,
Where the pallid yucca flowers once again;
And the dim coulees are furtive
With the coyotes slinking haste
While the branding fires are lit along the plain.

And the herds of ghostly cattle
Range beneath the quiet stars,
While the wary phantom riders circle wide;
Till they gather there in silence
To let down the misty bars
And corral the milling cattle safe inside.

And the shades of vanished bronchos
Plunge in rearing, snorting fright,
Shying wild-eyed on the brink of breaking day,
Till their reckless riders spur them
Into blind and panic flight,
When the eastern sky is slowly turning gray.

So the rattlers and the sage brush
And the riders disappear
When the sun climbs slowly up the eastern sky,
And the city's noisy clamor
Strikes anew upon the ear—
For once more the phantom round-up has gone by.

The Oil Fire

The lightning strikes, a sudden blinding flash
Of forkèd fire, a rending, tearing crash,
A deafening roar that shakes the very ground,
A sharp report, a sudden crackling sound!

The tank is struck! The mounting flames leap high
In wild fantastic light against the sky.
The strong steel crumples writhing in the heat
Twisting grotesquely, savage heat waves beat

In furnace blasts along the reeling air,
The oil fields lit and crimsoned with the glare
In wild unearthly beauty. Heavy, low
The black smoke hangs above the sullen glow

In rolling clouds with red flames bursting through
The whole earth has a lurid crimson hue,
The curious crowds that gather in to gaze
In half awed silence watch the great tank blaze

In devastating splendor. Far and wide
The sullen smoke hangs low on every side. —
The giant tank boils over, everywhere
A boiling flood of flame. The scorching air

Is blistering, blinding, seething torrents flow
In red cascades of flame. The savage glow
Of molten metal smoulders, twisted, scarred
The oil soaked ground is blasted, burned and charred.

All that remains to show the great fire's track
Is smouldering ruin, shriveled, seared and black.

The Knife-Thrower

The crowd is here, night after night,
Beyond the hard white glare of light,
Expectant faces, row on row,
To watch me while I poise and throw
The gleaming knives that cut the air
And, hissing, strike the rough boards, where
She stands with outstretched arms. The crowd
Sits rustling, murmuring aloud;
They watch the wicked knives that hiss
Like hooded cobras — If I miss! —
The long knives leap out, serpentwise,
Thin evil darts. Her laughing eyes
Are unafraid. I hem her in
With whizzing blades. A sudden din
Of swift applause goes sweeping by!
And every night I wonder why
My hand held steady. Will it be
The next night, with them watching me —
The next night, that my sure hand slips
And laughter leaves her painted lips?
The knife that, like a thrown thin flame,
Licks out and sears, will end the game?
The lean knives pin her to the boards,
And satisfy the eager hordes
That watch their vicious whizzing flight?
I wonder — will it be — to-night?

University

Could I remember ancient wars
When there were summer nights — and stars,
Could I unravel tangled rows
Of figures, when the picture shows
Were flashing out along the street,
And streams of music caught my feet
And wove around them shining strands
Of swift insistence, and my hands
Were full of moonlight cool and sweet?

One day a white fog drifted in
Across the campus ground,
The campus smothered in the mist
Was made of shadowed amethyst —
And changing opalescent light,
A world without a sound.
And when the sudden brass mouthed bell
Came startling me, I knew my lot
Was cast along unhappy lines.
I should have studied — and had not.

Could I go sleepless, day by day? —
Outside the hot white sunshine lay —
I saw raw copper sunsets blaze
On hammered anklets, and a maze
Of tawny fur, and gleaming eyes;
Great captive panthers, yawning, rise,
To purr against their burnished chains.
I woke — the vision yet remains —
My pained instructor's cold surprise.

One night the ukuleles sang
Beneath the purple sky,
And all the warm star-scented dark
Was full of wonder, and the spark
And glow of dreaming cigarettes
And fragrance drifting by.

And when the music faded past
I crawled into my iron cot.
The sleepy silence purred around.
I should have studied — and had not.

Could I go dragging chains of sleep
To early class, when I was deep
In dreams unshattered by the shock
And clamour of the wild-eyed clock?
Could I remember buried kings? —
I learned to blow pale spiral rings
Of hazy smoke; I learned the sway
And lure of syncopation's way:
I learned — so very many things.

One day the council summoned me
And said that I must go —
The atmosphere was bitter cold,
Their faces were like masks of old,
Like gargoyles made of carven stone —
My standards were too low;
In every class I failed to meet
Requirements, so they said, and yet —
How very strange — I learned so much,
And nothing that I will forget.

Heredity

Our apish forebears clung to trees,
In times far antedating these —
In sleep would cling with hands and toes.
They wore no high heeled pumps nor hose —
So Darwin says — I guess he knows.

If they had lost their hold, you see,
And toppled down from out their tree,
Wild animals were all around
To grab them when they hit the ground,
With teeth all primed and set to gnash,
Through cutlet, steak or fresh ape hash —
Careers were ended with a crash!

But those who wakened with a start
Did not become Ape á la carte,
They locked their toes in tighter hold —
The fit survivors, we are told,
Lived to become both gray and old.

We dream of falling, while in bed;
We waken with a start instead.
The instinct that our forebears knew
Is handed down to me and you.
We might have missed the whole Big Show
If Grandpa Ape, so long ago,
Had not waked just in time, you know.

The War Drum

I.
I have come down to watch them dance
With cool disdainful eyes.
It happens that by some strange chance
I have a strain of this same blood —
The great War Drum's unmeaning thud
Their savage, shrill barbaric cries
Amuse me oddly. Who could know
My own ancestors, long ago
Danced clay-daubed, shrieking, to and fro
For in my heart I mock them — so —
"Hai-ai!"

II.
The great War Drum goes thud, thud, thud,
The painted warriors shriek for blood,
The rattles shrill, the conches scream
Like devil blasts in some wild dream,
And through the clamor and the tumult comes
The blind uneasy throbbing of the drums,
A hollow, dull, reverberating sound
That echoes, muffled, from the very ground.

III.
These people must not guess nor know
My ancestry. My mocking air,
My wild derision — I must show
There never could be kinship there —
I wave my arms above the crowd
I mock these savages aloud —
"Hai-ai!"

IV.
Yet through my temples, pulsing, aching,
The blood beats thickly, throbbing, shaking
In blind vibration to the beat
Of sullen drums and stamping feet.
The wild flames throw fantastic rings of light
On paint smeared bodies. Thickly through the night
The maddening monotony of sound
Comes closing dully in from all around.

V.
The tumult shakes against my heart
Fierce and insistent, dull with pain
Prolonged and aching, through it all
The War Drum booms its sullen call
In fierce vibration through my brain —
A muffled pounding, thick, insane —
These are *my* people! Let me go!
You cannot understand nor know
That long-dead warriors call again —
Stand back! I join my tribesmen — so —
"Hai-ai!"

VI.
The great War Drum goes thud! thud! thud!
The Warpath shall run red with blood!
Back, though a thousand years have passed,
I come to join my tribe at last!
Shrilling exultant, till the savage sky
Rings with the echoes of our long war cry
I join the uproar, plunging to and fro!
The ghostly feathered braves of long ago
Wake shrieking, while the War Drum's maddening thud
Thunders above the tumult—Blood! Blood! Blood!

Robert

I.

I wonder what has become of Robert —
He was killed in the fighting in the Argonne
And buried there
Somewhere —

II.

But somehow I cannot think
That he is lying still in the ground
While the worms crawl through him,
That does not seem
Like Robert's way
Somehow —

III.

And yet — I cannot think he went to Heaven.
He used to wear those bright tan shoes
I hated so,
And he used to drink his coffee
Out of his saucer,
And get his thumb in it,
And he thought Mutt and Jeff
Were funny,
Not that that would make any difference —
Only—
He used to be cross to me
Lots of times
And he was always making fun
Of poor Mrs. Miller to her face
And so —
I cannot think he went to Heaven.

IV.

And still —
I cannot think he went to Hell,
He was always so good
To remember to bring things
From the store,

And once
He brought me a present
All the way
From Paducah,
A silk dress, red,
I could never wear it,
But still —
I cannot think that Robert went to Hell.

    V.
He was killed in the fighting in the Argonne
And buried there,
Somewhere,
But all the time
I keep saying to myself
I wonder what has become of Robert.

Sea Devils

When the fishermen spread out their nets to dry
    In the warmth of the Summer sun,
In the sweep of the wind 'neath the open sky:
Where the starlings wheel, and the seagulls cry,
They tell strange stories of days gone by
    And things they have seen and done.

They tell of adventurous, storm-tossed lives,
    Of days when they had to hew
The fog apart with their scaling-knives
    Till their fishing boats nosed through.

There were mermaids that fastened upon their lips,
    To suck out their dying souls,
There were winged sea-harpies that followed ships
    And lured them on to the shoals.

There were sea-born devils that lay in wait
    To capture their human prey;
They dragged them down to a terrible fate,
    Far off from the light of day.

They tangled the anchors and clogged the oars,
    They conjured the black storm clouds,
And ships were guided to devil-shores
    While devils wailed through the shrouds.

There are charms that the old witch-woman sells
    So the devils are kept away;
Though no one believes what the old crone tells
Yet they buy her pebbles and queer shaped shells,
And we learn to mumble her magic spells,
    For it's best to be safe, they say.

The Shark's Jaws

There was a chair in old St. Augustine
Of shark's jaws, set and riveted with steel,
A wishing chair. I laughed for I had seen
The others wishing gravely. I could feel
Their earnestness. I laughed and slid between
The heavy jaws, and found the luck was real.

    I found cool fronded palms in rows
    And warm, white, silver-scented nights,
    The streets a-stream with steady lights
    Of moving motors, and the shows
    A-glitter all along the street,
    And music sweeping like a sheet
    Of crested foam across the way
    From brilliant dance halls on the pier —
    The laughing, luring wonder, where
    The dancing couples cling and sway.

I idly wished for luck, and turned away.
I laughed because the strange, carved wishing-chair
Was worn smooth with many hands, the way
Some idol is worn smooth with kisses where
So many mouths have been. I turned to pay
The fee, and found luck followed me from there.

    I left a land of sullen rain —
    I found clear crystal sapphire days
    With red hibiscus all ablaze
    Between tall, feathered palms. Again
    I felt the lazy sunlight lie
    Across the days. The burning sky
    Was changeless wonder. I could feel
    The lure of roads that curved between
    Strange tropic jungles, and the sheen
    Of moonlight on a sea of steel.

The shark's jaws brought me luck—the warm, white sand,
The turquoise ocean breaking with a roar
Upon the shouting bathers hand in hand;
And casting up the surf boards on the shore;
The gay striped awnings, and the crashing band,
The jeweled shells along the white sea floor,
Laughter and warmth — a tropic wonderland
Of bright, fantastic beauty to explore.

Greenwich Village Nights

Beyond the glare of Broadway lights,
Up winding stairways, dark and steep,
Where strange fantastic shadows creep,
We find bizarre, exotic nights.

In dingy attics, where the air
Is thick with smoke, and semi-gloom
Fills every corner of the room,
The wind-blown candles flame and flare.

Impressionistic, clever scrawls
Of Spanish dancing-girls with fans,
Of pirates, Arabs, Mexicans,
Are sketched upon the whitewashed walls.

The girl from Main Street, freckled, lean
Poses with languid drooping gaze,
In imitation of the ways
Of vampire beauties of the screen.

Artists with vague impressive air,
And genius struggling to be free,
Chatter of art and anarchy
And shake their long untidy hair.

A creature with chalky, pallid skin
And green eyes glowing, sweeps the strings
Of some antique guitar, and sings,
Her sharp voice cracking high and thin.

Cruel and dangerous and soft,
Her green eyes prowl the smoke-filled air,
Stealthy and furtive, here and there,
Like cats that prowl a vacant loft.

Across the floor the dancers glide
The shadows leap, grotesque and tall
Across the grimy white-washed wall
They twist and slither, sway and slide.

The tourists jostle through the doors;
The eager crowds that search for thrills
Rush in across the dingy sills,
To jam the narrow dancing floors.

Among the softly shadowed lights,
Through realms of make-believe we stray,
Finding a strange fantastic way
Through restless Greenwich Village nights.

Chameleons (Manhattan Roof)

Between the palms are colored lights that play
In sweeping arcs of wonder, swing and sway
In dazzling circles where the dancers glide
Through flashing waves of splendor, brilliant eyed;
Through gorgeous crested seas of rapid light
Electric blue and incandescent white,
Through sudden crimson, orange, amber, chrome,
Prismatic splendors in a seething foam.

Chameleons within a sea of light
The dancers flash in iridescent flight.
Unreal, fantastic in a dizzy stream
Of rippling light, they turn and sway and gleam.

The brasses crash; the dancers sway and glide,
The eerie mockings of the trombone slide
Down changing scales. Through wave on wave of light
The dancers gleam, their faces oddly white,

Then weirdly blue, then sudden lurid green —
Chameleons with jeweled changing sheen,
The dancers shift and glitter, sway and glide.
The strange unearthly music seems to slide
Through realms of ghostly merriment unseen —
The doors of unreality swing wide.

The Walls of Ossining (Sing-Sing Prison)

There was a thin fine crystal rain
The night I came to Ossining.
It all comes crowding back again,
A soft spring night, a thin fine rain,
The jarring rumble of the train
And then — the walls of Ossining.

The great gray walls are grim and hard,
The prison walls of Ossining,
The rugged walls are bleak and scarred —
Outside I see the pacing guard,
The gray slag heap they call the year, —
The prison walls of Ossining.

Five years in striped captivity
Within the walls of Ossining, —
Through steel barred windows I can see
The Hudson running far and free,
In strong unfettered liberty
Outside the wall of Ossining.

*   *   *   *   *   *

Beyond the walls of Ossining
The bluebirds flash and dart and sing, —
And winter fades away in spring, —
We watch it here in Ossining.

City Born

Away from the noise of city streets
Away from the lights of town
Here on the lonely farm we watch
The black nights closing down.

The thick marauding darkness crowding close
Against the blank-eyed windows, all around
The stealthy waiting silence, vacant, vast,
Startled we hear the furtive creaking sound
Of wooden shutters straining in the wind.
The yellow lamp-flame sputters, flaring high
In smoky protest through the deepening gloom
And strange uneasy shadows fill the room
Formless and monstrous, crouching, furtive, sly
In silent menace while they wait to spring.
The blind wind, stumbling, groping, fumbles by
Sucking and mumbling with its toothless gums
At loosened clapboards like an ancient hound
It mouths and gnaws and worries at the eaves
Scratching and snuffing, circling round and round
In whining eagerness to dig its way
Through roof or wall and leap upon its prey.

We long for the hum of the busy streets
For the city's friendly roar
For the clatter and clang when the surface cars
Go by outside the door
For the night-hawk taxis that cruise the streets
For the clamorous days and nights
For the rattle and crash of the shuttling trains
—But the clapboards creak, and the wind complains
And only the loneliness remains
In place of the noise and lights.

1931-1940

PAUL KROEGER

Paul William Kroeger was born on March 20, 1907, in Guthrie, Oklahoma Territory, to John Maurice Kroeger and Lelia M. Shaw Kroeger, recent arrivals from Albia, Iowa, who built a home at 109 East Warner Avenue. Both parents had artistic backgrounds that heavily influenced their son: John was a musical accompanist who had studied at the New England Conservatory of Music in Boston and Lelia was a visual artist, singer, and poet who had taught art at Langston University when it first opened (then known as the Oklahoma Colored Agricultural and Normal University). Subsequently, the arts were never far from Kroeger's mind while growing up. As a child, he learned to play the piano and violin, and he also sang in the choir at St. Mary's Catholic Church and for local radio broadcasts. These interests continued into adulthood when he began building his own violins, designing his own grand piano, writing his own music and poetry, and collecting antique furniture.

Because he dabbled in music, religion, and literature throughout his life, Kroeger's poetic output was intermittent and sketchy. He never saw himself as just a poet and did not dedicate his life to the craft, once stating, "I am no poet, only a dreamer of dreams. I am Pan. I am the sad clown, wanderer in the wilderness." Despite these multiple sensibilities, Kroeger's poetic career began with an auspicious start. His first published poem, "Contrast," appeared in *Harlow's Weekly* on September 26, 1925, when he was just 18 years old. Six years later, at age 24, he sent his poem "Sonnet on International

Friendliness" to Governor William H. D. Murray who was so touched by its plea for world peace that he named Kroeger as Oklahoma's second poet laureate on August 18, 1931. This began a brief period of recognition for Kroeger's work; his philosophical poems on religion, nature, and love, which often employed allusions to music and musical instruments, began appearing in such publications as the *Anthology of Poetry by Oklahoma Writers* (which also contained two poems by his mother), *Harlow's Weekly*, and the anthology *Contemporary American Poets*. Some of his verse was also published in *American Poetry Magazine* under the pen name David Nash, and he had articles accepted to the *Christian Science Monitor* and *My Oklahoma*. During the 1930s, he was recognized as a significant figure in the state by being featured on Camille Nixdorf Phelan's Oklahoma History Quilt, which she presented to the Oklahoma Historical Society in 1935.

Upon being replaced as Poet Laureate by Jennie Harris Oliver in 1940, Kroeger quickly slid back into obscurity. Little is known about him today since he never published a book and since he did not leave behind a wife or children to carry on his legacy. He passed away in February 1977 in his hometown, largely forgotten by Oklahoma's literary community. He is buried with the Kroeger family in Logan County's Seward Cemetery. A simple gravestone marks his resting place.

Selected Bibliography

Primary Works
Caldwell Conner, Aletha. *Anthology of Poetry by Oklahoma Writers.* Guthrie, OK: Co-operative, 1935.
Paul Kroeger. "Oklahoma." Conner 15.
———, "Simile." Conner 16.
———, "To a Fly." Conner 16.
Kroeger, Paul W. "Contrast." *Harlow's (OK) Weekly*, September 26, 1925.
Nash, David. "The Dance." *Contemporary American Poets.* Ed. Horace C. Baker. Boston: Stratford, 1928. 150–51.

Secondary Works
Boren, Lyle H. and Dale Boren. "Kroeger, Paul William," *Who is Who in Oklahoma*. Guthrie, OK: Co-operative, 1935. 280–81.
Penn Cuff, Roger. "An Appraisal of the American Poet Laureates." *Peabody Journal of Education* 25, no. 4 (1948): 157–62, 164–66.
Marable, Mary Hays, and Elaine Boylan. "Paul Kroeger (David Nash)." *A Handbook of Oklahoma Writers.* Norman: U of Oklahoma P, 1939. 66–67.
"Pleases Governor; New Poet Laureate." *Gettysburg Times*, Sept. 15, 1931. 5.

Selected Poems by Paul Kroeger

Oklahoma

The red-bud, The black-oak, The white plum tree—
Spring was on the hillside, long ere Galilee.
The red man, The black man, The white man: Three,
Are buried on the hillside, but once in Galilee
The Good-man, The God-man looked across the sea
To the red-bud, The black-oak, The white plum tree.

Simile

My heart is like a violin
    That only you can play;
My heart is held securely in
    Your hands that gently sway.

Your dreams, the score; your words, the bow
    That makes my heart to sing . . .
Dream on, and whisper sweet words low:
    My heart more music bring.

The Dance
(To V. K.)

"On with the dance!" and the orchestra played.
Onto the floor couples glided and swayed.
Pivot and spin. Then away as on wings.
Slow now the step while the violin sings.
Orchestra! Revelry! Symphonic bliss!
"On with the dance!" May it ever be this!
Melody! Clarinet! Tempo gavotte!
Why think of sorrows and things that are not?

Solo! The trumpeter! Spotlight—and then
Silv'ry tattoo like the sunlight on rain;
Silv'ry tattoo like the twinkle of stars:
Beauty of Venus and brilliance of Mars . . .
Somebody whispers and wonders just why
Dances and music and starlight must die.
Cymbal! And tom-tom—a Cairo street
Comes to the mind 'mid the stamping of feet.

Rhythm of cymbals and pulses and drums,
Rhythm that livens and rhythm that numbs,
Rhythm that maddens the blood as rich wine,
Rhythm celestial and rhythm divine!
Then like a hush o'er Galilee hill,
Tom-toms are silent and cymbals are still.
Waltzing to whispering notes of the flute,
Deaf to all else are the dancers, and mute.

Deaf to all else but the unspoken peace;
Prayers in their hearts that the dance might not cease.
But, like the starlight, and too, like the rain,
Dances must end, nor the dancers remain.
Lovers must part, and the music must fade;
Song is forgotten, and memories made . . .
Mem'ries of dreams that are born of a dance;
Music, and laughter, and Beauty's romance.

But though the music be faded away,
Out of the stillness a voice seems to say,
"On, ever on with the dance, O my Heart!
Life is a highway and Love is a mart.
Pass it on by as you dance on your way;
Dreams will buy kisses, and kisses are gay . . .
Orchestra! Revelry! Symphonic bliss!
On with the dance! May it ever be this!"

Contrast

Tiny bluebird, at my window, tell me, tell me why
You do not fly higher, higher, far up in the sky,—
Higher, higher, ever higher in the blue-domed sky.

Think you! All the world's below, while, high above so far,
You go skimming, diving, climbing, like a speeding star,
Blending with the painted sky the blue flash that you are!

Is it not a greater thing, to fly high overhead?
Lo!—The golden eagle soaring with his wings outspread!
Why not up to share his joy, up from this earthly bed?

Hark to me, and I shall tell you: 'Twas not meant that I,
Tiny bird of tinted feather, should climb in the sky,
Higher, higher, ever higher in the blue-domed sky.

For, if I should climb beyond those clouds white as the dove,
Who could see my tinted plumage 'gainst the blue above?
Ah, none! And then, I would have lost my share of human love!

To a Fly

We were alone,
The fly and I,
In my small, square room,
And the light;
The light for the fly;
For me the gloom.

The fly
Did not know that I
Wanted to be happy too.
With impunity
I could have crushed him.
(I thought of it)
But I left him to the light
And the song of his merry wings.

Who knows
That in some other light
I shall not be left uncrushed,
Left to my own glad song
By One to be me
As I to the fly?

1940-1942

JENNIE HARRIS OLIVER

The best known and most commercially successful of the early poets laureate, Jennie Harris Oliver was born in Lowell, Michigan, on March 18, 1864, to George W. Harris, a fiery Baptist evangelist of Scots-Irish ancestry, and his wife, Mary Ann Walton Harris, a learned woman of English heritage. Although Jennie Harris's formal education ended after grammar school, she continued learning as a teenager by reading books from her father's library and by taking nature walks with her mother, who taught her about northern flora and fauna. In 1891, after George's death, the Harris family moved to Kansas before finally settling in the community of Shiloh in Oklahoma Territory, where the future author taught school. Here, she met her husband Lloyd Oliver, a cotton planter and gin owner. They married in 1901 and lived for most of their lives in the town of Fallis at the top of "the long red hill" on Stillman Avenue that the poet often mentioned in her work.

It was as a newlywed that Jennie Harris Oliver began her formal literary career, finding time to write stories for regional newspapers and *Sturm's Oklahoma Magazine* between her "biscuit making and dish washing." Encouraged by western novelist Vingie Roe, she eventually borrowed an old typewriter, a device that she had never used before, and began pecking out more professional-looking manuscripts upon manilla wrapping paper that she had ironed out smoothly and cut to the correct size. She considered her life to begin at this time: "no matter what privations, what disappointments, what sufferings—I had my charmed world to enter and close the door. Like teaching, it kept me young—oh, very young!" In 1908, the story "The House that Jack Built" (originally titled "The House Behind the Dogwoods") became her first national publication by appearing in the short-lived *Munsey's Live Wire Magazine*. For it, she received $10. This event began more than thirty years of publishing stories and poems in such large-circulation periodicals as *Holland's Magazine*, *All-Story*, *Woman's World*, *Argosy*, and *Good Housekeeping*. During the height of her career, Oliver earned more than five figures a year from her magazine publications.

Although her husband passed away in 1933 and her mother shortly afterward, this did not slow Oliver's productiveness. In 1934, her *Red Earth: Complete Book of Poems* were published by a regional company, eventually going into five editions, and in 1935 a collection of her Mokey Delano stories appeared, the rights of which were bought by Metro-Goldwyn-Mayer as a Jackie Cooper vehicle. The film eventually debuted in 1942, starring Donna Reed, Robert Blake, and Billie "Buckwheat" Thomas. In 1938, Oliver's second book of prose, *It is Morning*, was also published.

With such national attention came much regional recognition. Many Oklahoma college clubs and women's groups began inviting Oliver to read her poems, and she was granted an honorary membership into Guthrie, Oklahoma's Altrurian Club. In 1938, the city of Lawton celebrated a Jennie Harris Oliver Day, honoring her with a parade and banquet. Many authors also began trekking to the author's home each spring to meet her and to receive writing/publishing advice. In 1939, she was named to the Oklahoma Memorial Association's Hall of Fame. The following year, at the proposal of journalist Kenneth Kaufman in his "Book Page" column for *The Daily Oklahoman*, Acting Governor James E. Berry named Oliver the state's third poet laureate. By this time, however, Oliver's years of improper nourishment began weakening her bones, which greatly slowed her output. She first broke her ankle and then her back. Her final stories were written in collaboration with Joe Fitzpatrick, collected in the book *The Singing Hand*. She passed away on June 3, 1942.

Despite having been born and raised in Michigan, Jennie Harris Oliver fell in love with Oklahoma upon her move to the state in 1898. Subsequently, many of her poems, including "Red Earth," "Hail" and "Vingie E. Roe," deal with the state's landscape, weather, and people, illustrating both the difficult and joyous aspects of life on the southern plains. Because of this, she was the first poet laureate to commit herself fully to celebrating Oklahoma. As she noted in her final book, the autobiographical *Pen Alchemy*, "*I loved the Oklahoma Sun* . . . Summer is the time to write of lakes, pines, Indian pipes, ferns and mandrakes." Although much of her verse, like her stories, tended to be religious and sentimental—she often evoked pathos in readers by lending anthropomorphic qualities to animals and plants—their strength derived from her sincere depiction of the state's flora and fauna and the ways in which they fit with God's conception of the universe. Her influence was so important to other Oklahoma writers that future poet laureate Bess Truitt and her colleague G. Rossman used "Red Earth" as the title of their short-lived poetry magazine, which featured many of the state's poets. The Poetry Society of Oklahoma also created the Jennie Harris Oliver contest in her name.

Even though Oliver's poetry leaned toward the provincial, this did not stop her from receiving accolades from international writers. English novelist John Cowper Powys called her poem "Noon Trail" one of the finest American poems he had ever read while the Chancellor of Oxford University, Lord Halifax, wrote favorably to her about *Red Earth*. Critic Roger Penn Cuff noted in 1948 that Oliver made "Oklahoma's red land . . . so attractive that it seemed the gods must dwell there." Through her narrative and lyric poems, Oliver granted Oklahoma the attention it deserved both nationally and internationally, setting the stage for later, more accomplished poets laureate, all of whom owe her a debt of gratitude for making the state a worthy subject matter for contemporary poetry.

Unfortunately, the community of Fallis that Oliver so loved (and that served as home to such other writers as Vingie E. Roe, Aletha Caldwell Connor, and Cecil Brown) is now considered a ghost town, having been abandoned by both the Fort Smith and Western and the Katy railroads. Its post office and business district have been closed for decades, and the town is hard to reach via impassable roads. Although Oliver's house has been gone for many years, the property's wishing well still stands, a symbol of her importance to the state that she depicted so often in her poetry and fiction.

Selected Bibliography

Primary Works

Oliver, Jennie Harris. *It is Morning*. Kansas City: Burton, 1936.

———. *Mokey*. Kansas City: Burton, 1935.

———. *Pen Alchemy*. Oklahoma City: Dunn, 1939.

———. *Red Earth: Complete Collection of Poems*. Kansas City: Burton, 1934.

Oliver, Jennie Harris, and Joe Fitzpatrick. *The Singing Hand of Joe Fitzpatrick*. Oklahoma City: Dunn, 1939.

Secondary Works

Boren, Lyle H., and Dale Boren. "Oliver, Jennie Harris." *Who is Who in Oklahoma*. Guthrie, OK: Co-operative, 1935. 381.

Cuff, Roger Penn. "An Appraisal of the American Poets Laureate." *Peabody Journal of Education* 25, no. 4 (1948): 157–62, 164–66.

Marable, Mary Hays, and Elaine Boylan. "Jennie Harris Oliver." *A Handbook of Oklahoma Writers*. Norman: U of Oklahoma P, 1939. 25–28.

Morris, John W. "Fallis." *Ghost Towns of Oklahoma*. Norman: U of Oklahoma P, 1978. 80–81.

Truitt, Bess. "Jennie Harris Oliver." *Chronicles of Oklahoma* 22, no. 2 (1944): 138–42.

Wilson, Linda D. "Oliver, Jennie Harris (1864–1942)." Oklahoma Historical Society. Accessed December 19, 2013. <http://digital.library.okstate.edu/encyclopedia/entries/O/OL003.html>.

Selected Poems by Jennie Harris Oliver

Red Earth

Oh, do not seek this red land
Unless it be for staying—
   (The red, red earth the jealous gods
   Have alchemied for you!)—
And do not drink its red dew
With any thought of straying;
The gods have dyed its tawny waters, too.

Oh, do not seek this red land
Because its gold is flowing—
   (The black, black gold the jealous gods
   Have for their own to spend!)—
And do not turn a furrow
If you think you must be going;
Your feet will carry red-earth to the end.

Oh, do not seek this red land
When red-bud lamps are burning—
   (The rose-red lamps in leafless spring the gods
   go lighted by!)—
And do not seek affection
If you've any thought of turning;
For red-earth love will hold you till you die.

"Here" (Oklahoma)

Here are no stern deep snows and frozen rivers;
Here are few long, gray rains. We have the sun—
A summer so replete there is no telling
When it is done.

Here we have winter as a white face, smiling
And after it, the warm rain vanishing.
A night of wind, a day of wild bird singing,
And flowers spring.

We have the mountains, not too steep for climbing;
And we have canyons, not too deep to cross,
What we have planted, gods or man may harvest—
There is no loss.

And here the stars are very low, and friendly;
The moon is whiter than the one we knew.
If earth and streams are red, we have the skyline,
And *it* is blue.

Here is the soul of all that Nature promised;
New friends to know! new books to read and lend.
If Snow was mother, then the Sun is stepland—
A journey's end.

Noon Trail

It was so still, that silence languished for a whisper.
It was so hot that pale flame cowered on the mesa.
A vulture, in the palsied blue above a lone foothill
Reposed upon its silken couch of ether, dozing.
And all the twisted desert people mutely smouldered,
It was so hot—and still.

It was so clear that cities swam up out of nothing.
Tree shadowed ponds of silvery, lilied whiteness, glistened.
The mountains, poppy-bosomed on the monstrous hem of distance,
Withdrew their filmy veils of finest-woven purple
And leaned their naked shoulders to the raptured canyons—
It was so clear. So clear!

It was so grim, that danger tottered in its cavern.
It was so bleached, that whiteness groped its way, snow blinded.
Upon the pallid rock the lizards, flat and soundless,
Slid slowly eastward toward the promise of a shadow.
There was no place to kneel in all that shriveled vastness
That was so white—and grim.

The Desert's Cistern

I am melon-thistle cactus,
I am nature's wizard-cistern
In the long white days of summer
When the sands are like an oven;
When the wind, as leaping fire,
Whirls and crisps the dry bleached grasses.
With my thorn-troughs I am storing
Snow from off the far blue mountains,
Mist from off the south-bound river;
Dew and fog from out the mirage
Trembling 'twixt the two air layers.

When the rider on the mesa,
Faint and choking, parched and burning,
Reels and cowers in the long trail,
Lifts his pleading eyes to heaven
For the cloud that does not blacken,
For the rain that never whitens,
I am waiting just before him.
Ages there I waited for him!
He can hew my troughs that battled
With the dryness and the deadness;
He can cup my fleshy tower,
Drink, and go away rejoicing.

Courage

The lone pine clung to the arid rocks
Against the blast,
Its stooping shape was dwarfed and mean
It seemed to cast
A hateful scar on the sky and earth,
And no one guessed
That it sought to be what it had to be
On that bare crest.
For oh, the birds in their wild delight
Came nesting there;
The awkward shadow housed and homed
The timid hare.
The lone pine clung to the arid rocks
Discomfited—
The surly, lashing wind went by . . .
And shook its head.

The Ruined 'Dobe

In the sunlight and the moonlight,
In the low-hung desert starlight,
Stands an old forsaken 'dobe
Like a grim, distorted dream.
And its lidless eyes look westward;
The low ceiling sags and crumbles;
While bats hang down, like dusty rags,
From one long rafter beam.

In the old forsaken 'dobe
Lizards dart, all green and golden,
And the rattler trails its diamond length
Along the earthen floor.
And the old blind limping pinto,
Fumbling on the rocks and rubble,
In the fury of the sandstorm
Stumbles through the open door.

In the old, forsaken 'dobe
Coyotes sneak and barn-owls slither,
And the swoop of seeking buzzards
Haunts the pinion-scented air.
On the hearth, a ruby cactus blooms—
(A strangely-lighted candle)—
When the wind from off the mesa
Makes its petals flame and flare.

On a shelf within the 'dobe
There are cups of clay, soft colored.
There's a little wicker cradle,
And a thimble, and a glove.
While around the ruin, mountains,
Purpled by the wine of shadow,
Cast a wistful benediction
On a broken dream of love.

JENNIE HARRIS OLIVER

Dust

Dust lay so thick the lonely room was strangely shrouded
As robed in ghostly cloth no mortal hand had woven.
Dust lay so deep the mouse-folks planted steps like flowers,
And roaches fretted seams along its patterned surface;
While spiders, weaving tapestries upon the ceiling,
Let down their cloudy curtains on the dim-eyed windows.

Dust lay so thick her dearest books had felted covers;
The roses in a yellow bowl were quenched to powder;
Her empty shoes as shadows seemed to fade and totter.
The bed and chairs, and all her homey little dresses,
Were merely shapes; and underneath the coward mirror,
The shining beads she wore had turned as gray as ashes.

Dust lay so deep, where we had lived awhile, and parted,
It seemed as if a grave had closed upon our story;
But I found footprints all along the floor and stairway—
Dim little prints, as if the steps late trod were treasured
By a later dust; while on the surface of a table
Were traced in girlish hand, the precious words: "I love you!"

Hail

It hailed so fast that fugitives in jady armor—
The katydids, and bugs-of-June—were sadly broken.
It hailed so fast that rabbits died of heart failure.
A man and maid, both firmly pledged to lifelong hating,
Were chased beneath a bridge, among the bats and spiders.
There was no place to turn and flee one from the other,—
It hailed so fast.

It hailed so hard that birds were pelted from the wires.
The foxes and the wolves were stunned and almost done for.
The porcupines and bears were somewhat bruised and harried.
The old bridge swayed and leaned beneath its icy burden.
The man and maid heard their own hearts as hailstones thumping,
And clung and kissed, nor scarcely knew what they were doing—
It hailed so hard.

It hailed so long that early cabbages were sorely mangled,
And plushy roses all were cut to crimson ravelings,
It hailed so long that gold-fish perished in the fountain;
The baby's boarded playhouse fell and broke the tea-cups.
Beneath the swaying bridge life-hate had changed to rapture;
The winged god had blazed its way across the whiteness—
It hailed so long.

The Feathered Guard

The house martins flew to their homes in the west
And settled themselves in their cottage, to rest;
But one martin sat on the step in the sun
And watched the day die and the long shadows run.

He watched all the dangers that threatened below:
The boys with their missiles uplifted to throw;
A greedy cat with her green eyes alert;
A pig that was rooting its nose in the dirt.

But, deeply, he watched a black cloud in the sky
That put out the sunlight, and made the dust fly.
And when a storm broke he still clung in his place
With the hail on his back and the wind in his face.

His black silhouette could be seen by the night
When the thunder bolts rattled and lightning ran white;
His balancing wings tilted high, tilted low,
But his sharp little head ever turned to and fro.

And, as hour by hour, he clung in the storm—
The rain beating fast on his tremulous form—
Behind him, his people, so jealously kept,
Enfolded themselves in their feathers and—slept.

Orphans

The black bear searched the empty woods
Alone and starved and small
And all around him great bee-trees
Rose up, a silent wall.
And there were bogs and rotted logs
For a bearlet to rip and tear;
And there were berries cloying sweet
For a hungry bruin's fare.
But the small black bear was merely half
Of what a bear should be;
So he could only walk the woods
And whimper dolefully.

Last night he had slept in his mother's arms—
The shaggy arms of a bear;
Tonight he grieved as a cub will grieve
When the hunter has been there.

The gold bear searched the purple deeps
Of a brilliant autumn sky
While under his nose and under his paws
The silent earth went by.
The honey-bees of the Pleiades
The ants of the Milkyway—
And all of the silver fruits of the sky
Were clustered in night array.
But he had need of the Other Bear
That circled the empty blue—
The great gold bear that led him forth
When the universe was new.

He did not know why his trail was lost
From the trail of the Mother Bear;
He could only search as a cub will search
When the hunter has been there.

Lindbergh

Who are these that fly as clouds, and as doves to their windows?

Isa. LX–8

He left the earth and all the clans of pleasant grasses,
The homely roofs and shaggy trees and mountains,
He passed the singing lark and the sun-climbing eagle.
Where shapes of peering fog around him trooped, unresting,
And ice, as birds of passage, hung upon his going,
No lovely flowers of morning blossomed at his casement;
No torch of noon was there, nor wistful lane of evening.
No river dragged the stars along the shore of midnight:
Nor friendly children followed on his fluid pathway.
His home was a mirage—his mother's face, a dreaming.
But, where his courage was stayed on beams of thought and silence,
Wings, that were not wings, held fast the arc of nothing.

Between the pulsing Galaxy and soundless shadow
He found the way of death—an utter isolation—
A uselessness of earthly taste and smell and seeing;
That dearth of fellow hand and eye and pressing shoulder.
But . . . Comrade of the air; Columbus of new distance—
He spanned the "deep" alone!

The earth arose to meet him
As one bright form that housed the soul of Triumph:
And all the proud world waited at his open window.

Vingie E. Roe

For her, the sea and wind sang paeans wild,
The desert bloomed, the woods and mountains smiled.
A skein God wove her soul, of strength and fire,
Of love and mystery, and divine desire
To share the silent miracle—to give
Her hidden world its charmed life to live.

So, touched by inspiration's vivid gleams
Her soul awoke from music-haunted dreams.
She wrote: a magic thread was found:
Across the page her gold skein unwound.
Lo, stories sweet and keen as mountain air.
A-throb with mystery and love were there!

Souvenir

The necklace is not amber, fairest one,—
A miracle of glass; a frozen sun.
Old Woonah wove it, twined it for your throat.
Old Woonah's old! Time was when she could gloat
O'er fine quill chains as white as curdled milk,
And work strange dreams on doeskin soft as silk;
Memories of wood-smoke, birds, and roaming deer;
Of wigwam dance, the hunt, the changing year.

Old Woonah was a slim young maiden then,
And most desired by all the stalwart men.
It's hard to be an old, brown, shapeless crone
With eyes like beads that once as moonbeams shone;
And hard to see the Chief—Young Woonah's Brave—
Bring to the 'dobe hearth another slave,—
A lithe young thing, with children at her knee;
(My eaglets grew—they have forsaken me!)
Ah, buy the yellow necklace, fair one, buy,
It is not amber, but—one cannot die!

Hackberry Trees

When I went down to Waco—
To where my red earth ends,
It was the trees that welcomed me
With all their banners glowing;
That pinned my hair with moon and stars
And set their trumpets blowing
When I went down to Waco—
Down where my red earth ends.

When I went down to Waco
I found the trees my friends:
In every tree, a mocking-bird,
In every bird, a sonnet.
And oh, the berries green and cool
My black cape wore upon it
When I went down to Waco
And found the trees my friends.

When I went down to Waco—
(That's where my read earth ends)—
The dryads came and marched with me
In garments green and flowing.
Some little children saw us pass
And watched where we were going
In leafiest processional
Where my red country ends.

Oh, I went down to Waco
With sorrow in my breast.
The trees knelt down in purple shade—
I knew that they were praying.
And how the swift tears blessed my eyes
At what their lips were saying:
"We trees are here to comfort you;
And we are here—for rest."

1943-1944

DELLA I. YOUNG

When Jennie Harris Oliver passed away on June 3, 1942, the position of Oklahoma's poet laureate was left vacant until the following year when Della Iona Cann Young was appointed. Of the four poets who had served since 1923, Young was the oddest choice since she was known more as an educator and folklorist than as a poet. Unfortunately, little is known about her life today except for a few biographical facts that have been researched by family genealogists.

Della Iona Cann was born just north of Topeka in Holton, Kansas, on February 8, 1872, to Clark Mercer Cann, a farmer originally from Pennsylvania, and Zimenia Hulan Cann, his devoted wife. For the most part, the Cann family lived in Wabaunsee, Kansas, until Clark and his daughter took part in the Cheyenne-Arapahoe Land Run on April 19, 1892, having entered Oklahoma Territory from Texas. After filing his claim near the town of Cheyenne, Clark moved his family permanently to western Oklahoma. Two years later, Della Cann, who had been working as a teacher at Red Moon School, filed her own claim in Cheyenne, the town where she would eventually meet her husband, rancher and farmer Andrew Clyde Young. They married in Amarillo, Texas, on Christmas Day, 1906.

Although western Oklahoma was a desolate place, the region offered Della Young opportunities that she may not have received in more traditional, polite society, proving to be a good fit for both her tenacity and spunk. During her ensuing years as an Oklahoman, she was hired as the first school teacher in Grand County (later becoming county superintendent); she served as the principal of Cheyenne public school; and she later opened her own private subscription school (which closed after two months). It was here that she also gave birth to her three children: Frances Elizabeth, Marian Vashti, and Allison Clyde. Young's growing family, however, did not quench her enthusiasm for public service and her dedication to improving the lives of western settlers through education, which she tirelessly continued well into her seventies.

In 1943, Young was awarded the state's poet laureate position despite having published only two notable poems, "October in Oklahoma" and "To the Antelope," both of which were included in the anthology *Old Trails: Commemorating the Old Trails and in Recognition of the Poets Thereof.*

Her inclusion in this book, no doubt, derived from her local notoriety as a storyteller and folklorist of the 1892 land-run. Since 1912, she had served as secretary and treasurer to the Old Settlers Association of the Cheyenne and Arapahoe Country in front of which she gave the address "Early Days in Roger Mills County," recounting incidents experienced by original settlers. During the mid-1930s, she also worked on a book of short stories that chronicled the lives of cowboys, farmers, and ranchers in western Oklahoma. Although she passed away before its completion, her son Clyde Allison Young completed the manuscript and privately published it under the title *Grass*. She also received notoriety in history circles for having interviewed the last survivor of Custer's 7th Cavalry from the Battle of Little Big Horn.

Upon her death on May 16, 1948, western Oklahoma lost an important folklorist, one dedicated to conveying her memories of the western land-run and of the individuals who worked to settle its unforgiving land. Although little is known about her today, her essay "Names in the Old Cheyenne and Arapahoe Territory" is again available in J. Frank Dobie's *Texas and Southern Folklore*, which can be downloaded as a print-on-demand book. Della I. Young is buried in Cheyenne Cemetery beside her husband, close to the people whose lives she honored and chronicled throughout her adulthood.

Selected Bibliography

Primary Works
Clark, Alberta Guest, and Gladys Clifton, eds. *Old Trails: Commemorating the Old Trails and in Recognition of the Poets Thereof.* Sublette, KS: Publication of the *Sublette Moniter,* s.d.
    Young, Della I. "October in Oklahoma." Clark and Clifton 74–75.
    ———. "To the Antelope." Clark and Clifton 73.

Secondary Works
Cuff, Roger Penn. "An Appraisal of the American Poets Laureate." *Peabody Journal of Education* 25, no. 4 (1948): 157–62, 164–66.

Selected Poems by Della I. Young

October in Oklahoma

In autumn an Indian Princess
Comes riding, her brown shoulders bare,
The coppered bunch grass from the hillside
A war bonnet gay for her hair.

The wood ivy's scarlet ripe berries
Are rouge for her full silent lips;
A blanket of cured mesquite grass
Falls soft 'round her strong slender hips.

The blue and white corn, the Mondamin,
Bejewels her dark tined chest;
In bracelets of crimson dyed sumac
Are her summer tanned arms gaily drest.

She's fire in the smoke of the morning
That fills ev'ry canon and swale,
She's perfume of summer's wild flowers
That grew by the meadow and trail.

She rides in the leveling sun rays
Wide sweeping her dolorful hand,
And pours out the paint from her vials
In splashes abroad o'er the land.

The cottonwood catches the yellow,
The shin'ry the brown and the red;
The bronze falling on the pale peach leaf
Hears the murmur, "Dear Summer has fled."

The oakvine, the dogwood, the sumac
To claret have changed from their green;
The broom on the chocolate benches
In yellow trimmed bonnet is seen.

She rides, for November is coming,
To her tepee far up the red hills,
Where in winter from spectrum of sunlight
Her paint tubes with color she fills.

And none but me knows the shy damsel;
I trailed by her pathway of flame;
She lets me help stake her wild buckskin;
And whispers, "October's my name."

To the Antelope

In the caressing river's curve
The antelope race and bound.
Their white tails flag in the wind
To their twinkling hoofs' shrill sound.

'Round their necks like tippets gray
The storm clouds densely fold.
The plateaus' brown and green to hide
And winter's rime and cold.

Above the dust and fog
Their faces toward the light
They sport in the morning sun
Or the moon and stars at night.

And we who grope below
In the clouds and mist and rain
May lift our eyes up to the light
Like the antelope high on the plain.

1944–1945

ANNE R. SEMPLE

The most educated and poetically sophisticated of the early poets laureate, Anne Ruth Semple was born on June 9, 1900, to Charles Alexander Semple, an Ohioan of Scottish ancestry who moved to Indian Territory in the mid-1800s, and Minnie Pitchlynn, a member of the Choctaw nation whose grandfather, Peter (Snapping Turtle), served as its chief in the 1860s. Two years after Anne's birth, Charles was officially granted membership in the Choctaw tribe by the United States government since he had lived as a resident of the Choctaw Nation for forty years and had married Minnie in 1880, fathering ten children. Even though Anne grew up in the town of Caddo with both of her parents officially recognized as Choctaws, this did not stop her from experiencing a dual racial identity since she came from two distinct American heritages: she was proud to be named a Daughter of the American Revolution since she could trace her family tree to the mid-1700s, but she was also haunted by the death of two great-grandparents on the Choctaw Trail of Tears. Subsequently, the blended cultural traditions that her family exhibited colored Anne Semple's life academically, socially, and poetically until her death in October 1987.

Although her parents had passed away by the time she was twenty, this did not stop Semple's higher educational pursuits, which became the main focus of her life since they allowed her to explore the legacies of her ancestors. At age 32, she received her Bachelor of Arts degree in Education from Southeastern State Teacher's College (now Southeastern Oklahoma State University) in Durant, where she further developed her interest in literature. Later, her father's religion influenced her graduate work: she earned her master's degree from Austin College, a school affiliated with the Presbyterian Church in Sherman, Texas, and her doctorate from Oklahoma Agricultural & Mechanical College (now Oklahoma State University), where she wrote her dissertation on the history of Oklahoma Presbyterian College (OPC), which had been co-founded by the Presbyterian Church and the Choctaw nation to education Native American girls. In 1957, her dissertation was published as *Ties that Bind: The Story of Oklahoma Presbyterian College* some twenty years after that school had closed.

Upon completing her undergraduate degree in 1933, Semple worked diligently at writing poetry, publishing in such newspapers and periodicals as *Oklahoma Teacher, The Caddo Herald, The Arkansas Baptist, The Durant Democrat*, and *Harlow's Weekly*. In 1942, her only book of poetry, *Prairie-Born*, was published by the Kaleidograph Press. This volume illustrated Semple's literary sophistication by employing a wide range of classic forms from aphorisms to villanelles in rhymed and blank verse. While many of her lyric poems praise the virtues and beauty of prairie life, she also included religious poems that express God's handiwork in nature as well as narrative poems that related Choctaw folklore. One of the more experimental poems is "On the Prairies They Say," in which Semple arranges regional witticisms, folk sayings, epigrams, and weather prophecies into stanzas that express the beliefs and superstitions of prairie dwellers. Her most impressive poem, "The Death of Pushmataha," relates an ancestor's ambivalence towards death that he implores his tribe to accept as a part of life. Two years after the publication of *Prairie-Born*, Semple was named Poet Laureate of Oklahoma by Governor Robert Samuel Kerr for her realistic depiction of life on the prairie and for her celebration of its pleasures. She was the first Native American woman to be honored with the post.

Although Semple's poetic output slowed after the 1940s, she remained a steadfast, devoted teacher for the remainder of her life. While earning her doctorate, she taught at OPC and at Southeastern State Teachers College, her undergraduate alma mater. As a professor at both institutions, Semple concentrated her efforts in helping Native American students adjust to college life, founding Southeastern's first Indian Institute, which eventually morphed into the Native American Symposium that still exists today. For her efforts in supporting the educational pursuits of Native American students, she was posthumously awarded Southeastern's Heritage Award in 2009 for having "impacted the history of Southeastern in some unique way." This tribute, which occurred twenty-two years after her death, served as a touching capstone for one who was dedicated to helping those who lived on the Oklahoma prairie and to depicting their difficult experiences.

Selected Bibliography

Primary Works

Semple, Anne. *Prairie-Born: A Book of Verse.* Dallas: Kaleidograph, 1942.

————. *Ties that Bind: The Story of Oklahoma Presbyterian College.* Sl: Sn, 1957.

Secondary Works

Cuff, Roger Penn. "An Appraisal of the American Poets Laureate." *Peabody Journal of Education* 25, no. 4 (1948): 157–62, 164–66.

"SE to Present Heritage, Benefactor Awards During Homecoming." *Durant Daily Democrat,* October 2009. Accessed April 15, 2011. <http://w.w.w.durantdemocrat.com/pages/full_story/push?article-SE+to+present+Heritage-+>.

Selected Poems by Anne R. Semple

These are the Prairie Lands

These are the prairie lands—
Our sun-crowned lands where a kindly God
Has shaped the earth with master hands,
And left behind prophetic sod.

These are the prairie lands—
Our fertile lands where a richness reigns.
The sod will go when need demands
To make a place for growing grains.

These are the prairie lands—
Our living lands where a meadow queen
With seeds of grass her realm expands,
Till distance wears her elfin green.

These are the prairie lands—
Beloved lands where a field lark calls!
Oh, who pretends he understands
How beauty thus the heart enthralls?

Quandary

A song, a surging song, the sea
   Demands. To sing it were delight,
But prairie winds have sung to me,
   And won my love and troth. Despite
The lure of prairie songs, this plea
   Of buoyant, surging waves in flight
Bestirs my heart. Should I betray
My troth, would grief my joy outweigh?

Prairie Vastness

This land,
Where vastness walks
In stately grandeur across
Resplendent plains, has space for all
Who long to walk where vastness goes.

Prairie Lore

Beyond the field across the plains,
When prairie grass is amber tanned,
There comes the smell of autumn rains.

The bunching quail in orchard lanes
Have caught the scent the grass has fanned
Beyond the field across the plains.

Along with flocks of restless cranes,
Whose anxious wails disturb the land,
There comes the smell of autumn rains.

At dusk the clinging air remains
To form a wispy, yellow band
Beyond the field across the plains.

To men who eye the weather vanes,
And know to read a shifting hand,
There comes the smell of autumn rains.

The guinea-hen, as daylight wanes,
Protests so all may understand—
Beyond the field across the plains
There comes the smell of autumn rains.

On the Prairies They Say

A cloudy sky, as night draws nigh,
    With blue enough for patch and stitches
    To mend a pair of Dutchman's britches
Will clear, they say, by dawn of day.

———

A sun-dog at sunset
Is the worst sign yet.
If you meant to rake your hay,
You'd better wait another day.

———

A storm of rain goes in the wake
Of fresh-made tracks of a garden snake.

———

No matter what your need or belief,
To sweep at night will bring you grief;
If sweep you must, be sure you're able
To leave some food on the kitchen table.

———

A warm, damp winter is sure to bring
Destructive storms in early spring.

———

Heat in winter—
Cold in spring—
The year's no good
For anything!

———

When tree frogs croak an' sing together,
It's sure to bring hot, dry weather.
If ole man tair'pen needs a soakin',
Whip th' frogs, an' stop their croakin',
For, if you stop their noisy song,
A rain will fall th' whole day long.

———

For sores that ache and throb with pain,
Just mix up dirt and cool, spring rain.
Apply this mud as thick as dough,
And soon you'll see your misery go!

———

When cow-flies bite,
And swarm at night
To buzz before
The kitchen door,
A storm may light
Before daylight!

The Caddo Hills

The Alleghanies touch the eastern sky;
Far to the west the lofty Rockies lie;
And these have heights to awe the hearts of men—
But should I name the hills I love, why, then
My thoughts would rush to claim the range which fills
My prairie heart: the low-flung Caddo Hills!

Luminous

Magnolia blooms are lustrous white
    Beneath a mist of crystal dew!
Arrayed in filmy, star-spun night,
Magnolia blooms are lustrous white.
When lambent petals catch the light
    My raptured heart cries out anew—
Magnolia blooms are lustrous white
    Beneath a mist of crystal dew!

Dancing Thieves

A band
Of gypsy leaves
Went dancing in the sunset
Aflame with colors which they took
From sunset's store of burnished gold.

The Clearing

The Washita withdrew from sight, and dared
    To show the grief she felt to see the sun
Whose touch disrobed her banks. Here moss despaired
    Of life, and dying vines were all undone
With shame and nakedness. What had been won
    Of loveliness was gone. She shrank from heat
Whose flaming hand the wood-things fear and shun.
    Bereft, replete with shame, but not defeat—
She waited there for rains to make revenge complete.

The Young Fisher and Grandpappy Crawdad

Crawdad, crawdad,
 Looky quick!
Fat bait, lean bait—
 Take yo' pick.

Ole man fish-ah,
 T'aint fo' me!
Go 'long, go 'long—
 Leave me be.

Crawdad, crawdad,
 How yuh feel?
Wake up, wake up—
 H'ya's yo' meal.

Ole man fish-ah,
 Hush, Ah say!
Run home, run home—
 Go yo' way.

Crawdad, crawdad,
 Hush yo' mou'f!
Come up, come up—
 Stop dis drou'f.

Ole man fish-ah,
 Hush, oh, hush!
Ah smells de 'fume
 O' cawn meal mush.

Crawdad, crawdad,
 Is dat so?
If you smells mush,
 Ah got t' go!

Ole man fish-ah,
 While yuh snacks,
Ah'll dig mah hole
 T' Halifax!

The Death of Pushmataha

Choctaw Lore: Pushmataha was a noted Choctaw chief who died in Washington, and was buried there with military honors.

Pushmataha knew the end was near,
But feared no thought of death and dying.
He called his tribesmen to his bedside,
And spoke with strength and feeling.
"The time will come to turn your footsteps homeward
But I shall stay, remaining here forever.
As you travel through the woodlands,
My brave young kinsmen there will say,

'Hear the sighing as the wind blows?
 Hear the pines their grief outpour?
Hear the bird call? Yes, she knows—
    Pushmataha is no more!'

The eager Indians there will ask you:
'Where is he who leads the Choctaws?'

When they question, end their wonder—
    Say the oak that heretofore
Lived to shade them, fell with thunder!
    Pushmataha is no more!

Comfort them who dread to hear it—
    Hear the crashing, hear the roar.
Tell them calmly, lest they fear it—
    Pushmataha is no more.

I, who know how Choctaws suffer,
Must not stir their hearts to grieving.
When you see them say with kindness—
Pushmataha is no more!"

He looked to see who all were present,
Smiling bravely as he named them.
"Brothers, now I leave you—
Pushmataha is no more!"

They, who left his bedside, found he spoke
As one who sees tomorrow's sun.

———

When Choctaw mothers teach their children,
And aged Indians think of death,
They tell of Pushmataha,
Who died as they would die.
With vibrant voices, low and deep,
They speak with brave and deathless pride:
They tell of Pushmataha,
And ever ends their story—

"Thus, the Choctaws speak of dying;
  Thus, we mourn, and death deplore.
Simply, thus, we say with sighing,
  'Pushmataha is no more!'"

1945–1963

BESS TRUITT

Born in Madison, Iowa, on June 3, 1884, Bessie Belle Truitt was the daughter of Joseph Otterbein Truitt, an easterner from Ohio who started moving west in the early 1880s, and Annie Bell Starkey, an Iowan seven years his junior. After their marriage on June 7, 1883, the couple remained in Iowa for several years until they relocated to Kansas in the late 1880s. However, in 1893, the family finally settled in Enid, Oklahoma Territory, having taken part in the Cherokee Outlet Land Run on September 16th. It was here that Bess Truitt lived for most of her life, never marrying. Like other settlers at the time, the Truitts aspired to a complacent, middle-class lifestyle with Joseph working as a weighmaster and proprietor, Annie running a boarding house, and their four living children receiving an education. After graduating from Enid High School in 1901, Bess Truitt worked as a teacher in a one-room school for several years. In 1907, she attended Valparaiso University and six years later the University of Utah. In 1932, she finally graduated from Enid's Phillips University with a Bachelor of Arts degree and two years later with a Master's degree in Education. In the interim she had worked as Garfield County's Court Clerk, as a travel agent, and as a teacher in Oregon and Utah. In all, she taught for thirty years, seventeen in the Enid public schools. She also taught night classes to help immigrants obtain their citizenship after having worked for Oklahoma's Department of American Citizenship in the mid-1920s.

Although Truitt didn't seriously publish her verse until she reached her fifties, she was active in Oklahoma's literary community throughout her life, eventually serving as president for three organizations: the Oklahoma Poetry Society, the National League of American Pen Women, and the Enid Writers Club. For several years, she also edited the newspaper column "Port o' Poets" that was published throughout the state. Like most of her contemporaries, Truitt's poems and essays appeared in regional magazines and local newspapers. Some of her work also appeared in such collections as Aletha Caldwell Connor's *Anthology of Poetry by Oklahoma Writers* (1935), Anita Browne's *Anthology of the General Federation of Women's Clubs* (1936), and Franklyn Pierre Davis's *Anthology of Newspaper Verse* (1937). Even though these books lent Truitt a wider audience, she was never able to build a stable readership outside of Oklahoma.

Because of the hard work and dedication she lent to her writing, the 1940s proved to be the most productive decade of Truitt's literary career. In December 1940, Kansas City's Burton Publishing Company issued her first and only book of poems, *Thistle Down and Prairie Rose*, which contained a wide array of verse: imagistic nature poems, sentimental poems about mothers and children, religious poems, and historical poems about Oklahoma. The most impressive and experimental work in the volume, "Land Rush," depicts the exuberance of "Ten thousand men . . . risking their lives / For a patch of sun-soaked prairie earth" while battling wind, dust, glare, and exhaustion during a summer land run. Another notable poem, "In Fee," presents a settler who takes comfort in the diverse memories he has of the 160 acres he now must sell. Throughout the volume's four sections—entitled Moods, Portraits, Seasonal Cadences, and Laughter Patterns—Truitt explores the people and places that influenced her work and colored her life in Oklahoma. Because of her enthusiasm, many of the volume's poems were broadcast by various Oklahoma radio stations throughout the decade.

A year before *Thistle Down and Prairie Rose* appeared, Enid, Oklahoma's Commercial Press published *Range Rhymes and Recollections*, a book of cowboy stories, ballads, and poems that were edited by Truitt in order to "preserve the folklore of the plain in song and story and to present to our readers the spirit of the 'last frontier.'" Most of the stories and poems had been either previously published in *101 Ranch Magazine* (the official publication of the Cherokee Strip Cow-punchers Association from 1925–1927) or composed by members of the Chisholm Trail Memorial Association, of which Truitt was a member. The ballads included were transcribed by her while such cowboys as Frank Eaton (Pistol Pete) and Rolla Goodnight (Texas Slim) sang them. To show its appreciation for the book, the Chisholm Trail Association used the proceeds from its publication to support a fund to erect a monument just north of Enid that marked a point on the trail. Highly collectable today, *Range Rhymes and Recollections* succeeded in its purpose to document "the great cattle empire of Oklahoma" and the trail that the cowboys followed to bring their herds to market, a vanished world that saddened Truitt, who remembered the cowboys and land-runs of the late 1800s. Her dedication to the memory of the area's settlers continued with the *Journal of the Sons and Daughters of the Cherokee Strip*, which she edited for ten years.

Besides collecting cowboy literature, Truitt spent the mid-1940s championing the work of contemporary mid-western poets by co-founding *Red Earth Poetry Magazine*, which she helped to edit from 1944–1948. Having named her journal after a poem by Jennie Harris Oliver, a mentor who had supported her literary efforts, Truitt also wrote a eulogy of Harris Oliver for the *Chronicles of Oklahoma* that appeared in 1944, two years after the former poet laureate's death. A year later, Truitt herself became the state's poet laureate, having been appointed by Governor Robert Samuel Kerr to a one year term like her immediate predecessors Della Iona Cann Young and Anne Semple. However, since Kerr did not appoint another poet laureate during his last year in office and since the state's four succeeding governors failed to name another to the post, Truitt was generally considered Oklahoma's Poet Laureate during the 17-year interim until Delbert Davis's appointment in 1963. Subsequently, her eighteen years in the position ties with Maggie Culver Fry's for being the longest. Even after Davis's appointment, Truitt was named Poet Laureate Emeritus of Oklahoma for her dedication to advancing the state's reputation in poetry. She also had three poems published in the *Oklahoma State Senate Journal* in 1963 for depicting "the hopes, aspirations, trials and triumphs of our people."

Despite serving as Oklahoma's poet laureate for this long amount of time, Truitt's productivity declined after the 1940s due to her old age. Although she continued to write poems and essays during the 1950s and 1960s, she never recaptured the attention she received during the 1940s. In 1959, however, she was honored by being named to Oklahoma's Hall of Fame and to Who's Who of American Women. In 1966, she was also given a Pride of the Plainsmen Award by Enid High School for her service and commitment to the Enid area. She passed away on August 20, 1972, at the age of 88 and is buried in Enid's city cemetery.

Selected Bibliography

Primary Works

Truitt, Bess. "Jennie Harris Oliver." *Chronicles of Oklahoma* 22, no. 2 (1944): 138–42.

————. "A Teacher's Plea." *Oklahoma Today* 13, no. 4 (1963): 9.

————. *Thistle Down and Prairie Rose*. Kansas City: Burton, 1940.

Truitt, Bess, ed. *Range Rhymes and Recollections*. Enid, OK: Commercial, s.d.

Secondary Works

"Bess Truitt's Poems Entered in Journal." *Enid Morning News*, May 25, 1963. 5.

Cuff, Roger Penn. "An Appraisal of the American Poets Laureate." *Peabody Journal of Education* 25, no. 4 (1948): 157–62, 164–66.

"Miss Truitt, Seven Others Honored at OC." *Enid Morning News,* November 17, 1959.

"Poet Laureate Emeritus Bessie Truitt Dies." *Enid Morning News*, August 21, 1972.

"'Prairie Rose and Thistle Down,' By Miss Bessie Truitt, Published." *Enid Morning News*, December 15, 1940.

Pyle, Wanda. "Who's Who Lists Three Women." *Enid Morning News*, January 16, 1959.

"'Range Rhymes' Published by Enid Teacher." *Enid Morning News*, September 10, 1949.

Selected Poems by Bess Truitt

Land Rush

Heat
> *Glare*
>> *Thirst*

Pittiless lash of a southwest wind,
Burning the restively shifting lines,
Land-hungry hordes, weary and worn,
The sharp staccato of army carbines.

Dust
> *Heat*
>> *Glare*

Drumming of hoofs on the sun-baked earth,
Rumble and roll of many wheels,
Uproar of voices excited and high,
A multitude charging in frenzied haste,
This pageant of hope and fear reveals.

Heat
> *Dust*
>> *Fear*

Smother of dust, agalloping team,
A man and a woman, half afraid,
A cluster of "young-uns," unkempt, forlorn,
A gaunt hound dog whose red tongue lolls
As he trots in the wagon's meager shade.

Glare
> *Dust*
>> *Heat*

Teams plunge on at maddening pace,
Eyes narrowed against the hot sunlight;
Ten thousand men are risking their lives
For a patch of sun-soaked prairie earth,
A claim in the "Strip" before the night.

Grit
  Dust
    Heat
A moving dust-wall, and nose to nose,
Speeding, the caravan madly races;
A broken axle, a splintered shaft,
A surcingle snaps, a rider falls,
A sulky lurches, rending the traces.

Dust
  Din
    Reward
Out of the moil of dust and confusion
Emerging a commonwealth on the plains;
Homes for the fearless frontier fighters,
Pioneers all, scorners of ease,
Iron of endurance flows in their veins.

Time

Today's
Memory and
Tomorrow's dream
Embracing the past with
Remembrance and the future
With longing.

Symphony

Children's laughter, youth's romancing,
Dreams of homes with love complete;
Bright, the gay allegro movement,
Virile, calm and strangely sweet.

Dull, the largo, ever pounding
On the wheels in marts of trade,
Long established by tradition,
Church, and laws to be obeyed.

Now, the plaintive notes of minor,
Dark with sin and pain and fear,
Misery of unemployment,
Sickness, sorrow, death appear.

Each of us a part as player,
Fashioning his destiny;
As the maestro sets the tempo,
Writes the score in changing key.

April Love

A flame
With fire divine
Of new-born love,
A young heart shivers and
Dissolves—Soft eager eyes stare
Unseeing.

Marriage

Marriage
Is a oneness
Of apartness.
Like lute strings quivering
As the winds of heaven dance
Between them.

Children

Children
Are the living
Arrows sent forth
From the parent bow: Sons
And daughters of life's longing
For itself.

Talking

Talking
Murders thinking.
You delight in
Your lips when you cannot
Longer dwell in your own heart's solitude.

Mid-summer

This is the golden season of the prairie
The sun lies amber on a stretch of grass,
The field mice peep from roots of coral pinkness
And yellow flowers bloom in clustered mass.

A veil of haze that seems to float and settle
Wears opal tints of summer mists in early morn;
And there are half-heard sounds within the orchard
As afternoon with ripeness fills her horn.

Comes now the quiet of the prairie evening
Its silence is a melody set free,
Nothing is apparent in the shadows
Except a star, low-hung, above a tree.

A Villanelle

A wonderful tree, the giant pine—
Stately and proud as a warrior bold;
Trim and perfect in every line.

Around its base, when the moon's benign
Dance tiny dryads gray and old,
A wonderful tree, the giant pine.

Great strength and beauty here combine
With art, its symmetry to enfold;
Trim and perfect in every line.

Displaying a grandeur, quite divine
In quivering boughs, all thunder-rolled
A wonderful tree, the giant pine!

Its spicy odors revive, like wine
When sipped from a cup of beaten gold,
Trim and perfect in every line.

For pomp of winter, dryads design
Robes of ermine against the cold,
A wonderful tree, the giant pine;
Trim and perfect in every line.

November

Gray skies—
Birds winging south
Robbing late fields;
Nights sharp with frostiness
Offer no condolence to
Trees bereft.

A Teacher's Plea

Dear Father, hear me as I pray
For every child I teach today:
That each small face may be to me
A cherished photograph of Thee;

With patient sweetness, let me guide
Each precious soul with love and pride.
That when I make their record sheet
No space may be left incomplete.

Then grant me grace, each mind to give
A clear-marked rule by which to live;
And then, dear Father, I beseech
That I may keep the rule I teach.

Maids of Yesterday

When you and I were little girls,
We wore our hair in long curls,
Or braided tight in pig-tails two
And tied with ribbons pink and blue.

We did not wear bright-hued half-sox
For mothers suffered direful shocks
If one had dared to show her knees—
It mattered not how strong the breeze.

Our dresses buttoned down the back,
The skirts were full, there was no lack
Of cloth, to make them high of neck,
Or long of sleeve our arms to deck,

We wore real petticoats you know
To keep us warm, and not for show;
When you and I were little girls
And wore our hair in braids and curls.

Secrets

Secrets—
Spicy morsels,
Whispered softly
Into the ears of friends—
For all the world to know and
Talk about.

In Fee

I sold the hundred and sixty,
Delivered the deed today;
But nothing was said of the wood thrush-song,
    Or the light that softly lay
    On the rim of the open prairie,
    Or the fragrance of new-mown hay.

    It did not include the transfer
    Of the wind's low symphony
    Idly swinging the nests of birds,
    That hang in each maple tree;
    Or the title to love and service.
    All these, I hold in fee.

1963–1965

DELBERT HUGH DAVIS

Like many of his predecessors, Oklahoma's seventh poet laureate, Delbert Hugh Davis, was not a native Oklahoman. Born in Lockwood, Missouri, on June 1, 1883, to parents with eastern roots—his father was from Illinois and his mother was from Virginia—Davis came to the Oklahoma Territory by covered wagon at age six in 1889, settling with his family in the community of Mulhall, a small train stop on the Santa Fe Railroad line in the north central part of the territory. At age eight, Davis moved 25 miles away to what became Cimarron Township in Logan County after his Uncle Jesse Henley made a claim when the Iowa Reservation was opened for white settlement. Here, Davis lived with his Uncle Jesse, Aunt Hester, and cousins Nannie, Donald, and Gladis until age twenty when he moved to Stillwater to complete the eighth grade, the last of his formal education.

During his twenties and thirties, Davis lived in New Mexico and Wyoming, where he worked as a horse wrangler and stage coach driver. Upon returning to Oklahoma, he earned a third grade teaching certificate and taught elementary school for thirteen years, having settled in Logan County's Iowa Township with his wife Ernestine and their children, Roaine and Living. During World War II, Davis lived two-and-a-half miles southwest of Gravette, Arkansas, where he and his family farmed for a living. Always feeling the pull of his adopted home state, however, he eventually returned to Oklahoma, settling in town of Wellston. Here, Davis fell in with the literary community of nearby Fallis, whose members supported and nurtured his love of poetry. While living here, Davis was named Oklahoma's seventh poet laureate by Governor Henry Bellmon in 1963. Two years later, on July 20, 1965, Davis passed away in Wellston while still serving in the position.

Because of his farming and ranching backgrounds, the subject matter of Davis's poetry often concerns the seasons; nature; animals; cowboys; and personal, sentimental topics. No doubt, his experience as a third grade teacher also influenced his child-like verse, which employs hard-rhymes, end-stopped lines, and regular rhythms as well as his depiction of western stereotypes. Since he worked as a laborer all of his life, he came to writing poetry late, self-publishing his only book, *Pipe Dreams,* at age 69 in 1952. This, when coupled with the fact that he rarely published his poems in magazines or journals, makes his appointment as poet laureate puzzling. The preface of *Pipe Dreams* shows Davis's inexperience and naïveté about writing poetry, which affected his ability to serve the position well: "[m]y objective [with this book] was to find out if anybody would care to read what I could write [. . .] The reason? I find quite a lot of pleasure in word juggling. Trying to join them together some how to make them readable." Although his verse was labeled as "folk poetry" by *Oklahoma Today* magazine in order to legitimize its simpleness, Davis's verse often comes off as sophomoric and sentimental to modern readers. Because of this, Delbert Davis is the least memorable of Oklahoma's poets laureate.

Selected Bibliography

Primary Works
   Delbert Davis. *Pipe Dreams*. Guthrie, OK: Calkins, 1952.

Secondary Works
   "Folk Poetry of Delbert Davis," *Oklahoma Today* 14, no. 1 (1964): 30–33.
   Greenfield, Gerry Stanfill. "Wellston." *Encyclopedia of Oklahoma History and Culture*, Oklahoma Historical Society. Accessed May 4, 2013.http://digital.library.okstate.edu/encyclopedia/entries/W/WE011.html.

Selected Poems by Delbert Davis

My Baby
   Dedicated to Roaine, My Daughter

A cherished Christmas present she
I see now looking back
Upon the night, when we received
A precious little pack of loveliness,
All pink and white, so like a tiny flower,
She nestled in her little bed.
Grew dearer every hour.
Like stardust falling in the night

She lighted up our home
With baby coos and childish laugh
That all too soon have flown.
And yet grown now to womanhood
She still remains the same,
Dear baby girl who on my heart
Must always have a claim.

The Sandpiper

There are sea faring birds
Bold nomads of the sky
That fly o'er the broad ocean's reach
But most cunning of all
Is the quaint little guy
Sand piper who lives on the beach.

That small busy body
Belongs to the sea
Wears feathers like other wild braves
Bread winner that lives
On the fringe of the surf
Long shoreman and child of the waves.

He salvages food
From the water washed sands
Where the spent waves come in and retreat
He darts in and out
From the rocks to the surf
So persistent on swift little feet.

His tiny legs twinkle
In rapid retreat
From the wavelets that roll into land.
What a long slender beak
What a queer little squeak
As he spikes for his food in the sand.

A serious minded
Alert little guy
Too busy to have any fun,
Trails the ebb to the sea
Leads it back to the rocks.
He spends most of his life on the run.

Graveyard Gossip

They was me, an' Ard, an' Berk, an' Ace,
Fox, Mike, and Blaika, an' Ott.
Grave diggers at the Cross Roads' place
Worked some an' talked a lot.

"Speakin' of skeery things," sez Berk.
"An' things that hurt like whiz,
The scorpion kin do real work
With that 'ere tail of his."

"He knows jest how to do his trick;
I'll bet a pair of mules
He'd chisel through a yard of brick
An' never whet his tools."

"The bumbly bee's a croonin' bold
Deceivin' thing," sez Ard.
"He's light and airy as the wind
But, boy, he sets down hard."

"Bees stung our yearlin' baby's foot—
Don't say it didn't swell!
By noon she couldn't wear my boot,
An' I wear number twelve."

"I hate a hornet, too" sez Mike,
"Above all other things.
A glimpse of one an' I am like
A monkey on a string."

"A hornet stung me on the thumb
While I topped corn, an' zounds!
I climbed the cornstocks one by one
An' jumped out on the ground."

"I dread a santypede, I guess,
The most of all," sez Fox.
"They'll steal yer entire skeleton
An' hide it in the rocks."

"You wake up feelin' sorter cramped
An' somewhat shocked, of course,
To find yer bony system vamped
An' suein' fer divorce."

"The ticks," sez Ace, real quiet-like,
"Et ever' bloomin' horn
From them 'ere speckled steers of mine
While I was plowin' corn."

Flying Saucers

We heard from, corner grocery stores,
Restaurants and dairy barns,
From city streets and radios,
Strange, wild, fantastic yarns.

Of bold space riding buccaneers,
Who sailed among the stars,
A million miles perhaps or more
From, some where out on Mars.

Half man, half wolf, but monsters, all;
Marauders to our world;
As swift descending thru the clouds
Their flying saucers whirled.

They came to clutter up our works
And meddle in our wars,
To steal our plans for atom bombs
And blow out all the stars.

But tearing up the Milky Way
By chesty Marrians
Is out of order; Such great work
Is for Americans.

'Twas, un-American at best.
Pro-Russian, at the worst,
To doubt, what any one had seen.
Dispute it, no one durst.

But every bubble bursts in time;
The Marrian saucers broke,
Now, some imaginative soul,
Can find another joke.

Evening at Lake Hiwassie

'Tis evening now—From wooded hills
The lengthened shadows trail
And wearied earth assumes a drowsy mood
As yonder in the valley
Half asleep and half awake
Hiwassie lies in quiet solitude.

Yon evening sun receding
Like a pretty golden hub
Those red and violet clouds but half reveal
With yellow, red and purple shafts
Like brightly burnished spokes
Creating there a vast and fiery wheel.

The lustre of the evening sky
Is mirrored in the lake,
In varied colours while I stand aloof
And watch the lazy motion
Of the dreamy sun-lit waves,
Like painted shingles on its liquid roof.

1966–1970

Rudolph Nelson Hill

Although many researchers list Arkansas as his birthplace, Oklahoma's eighth poet laureate, Rudolph Nelson Hill, was actually born in Protem, Missouri, close to the Arkansas border, on April 4, 1903, the eldest of his parents' four children. Both his father, Clarence Leroy Hill, and his mother, Elsie Keesee Hill, were natives of Arkansas, which may account for this common biographical mistake. As a small boy, Hill moved with his family from a cabin in the Ozark Mountains to the plains of south central Oklahoma where they drifted between Seminole, Wanette, and Konawa before finally settling in the town of Wewoka.

Showing an interest in reading as a young child and illustrating an especial talent for writing, Hill began dabbling in poetry at age 11. By the next year, he had written his first "official" poem, a rhymed Christmas verse entitled "Kris Kringle." By age 15, he had already become a professional writer by selling lyric poems to Chicago's *Mother's Magazine*. Such studiousness and determination was also typical of his academic work. While at Wewoka High School, he won an oratorical contest, and, as a senior, was named valedictorian of his class. Subsequently, he was accepted as an undergraduate student into The University of Oklahoma.

While at university, Hill's interest in writing continued. Here, he won his first poetry prize, which earned him $10 and saw the poem published in the *University of Oklahoma Magazine*. On campus, he was also made a member of Blue Pencil, the university's honorary organization for writers. The effect that these experiences had on Hill cannot be underestimated. For the rest of his life, he submitted poems to countless literary contests, winning many, and joined several state and regional literary clubs, eventually holding important positions in most.

Upon earning his Bachelor of Arts degree from OU on June 8, 1926, Hill returned home to Wewoka, where he lived for the rest of his life. Here, he worked as a stenographer, school teacher, and court reporter before becoming a lawyer in 1931. However, during this time he never gave up on writing, placing his poems in such periodicals as *Harlow's Weekly*, *The New York Times*, and *The Daily Oklahoman* and in such anthologies as *Contemporary American Poets* (1928) and *Choir Practice* (1933). He also began a short-lived venture publishing his own magazine, *Barking Water*, which he found too costly and time-consuming to continue.

In 1929, Hill self-published his first book: *Red Ship Wings: Poems*, printed by the Lasiter Printing Company in Wewoka. For the most part, this volume set the template Hill would follow in his later books. It contains poems on romantic, sentimental, religious, patriotic, and western themes written in conventional literary forms that rely heavily on hard, end-stopped rhymes with monotonous rhythms and meters. Many times, Hill undercuts his interesting subject matters with trite poetic conventions and forced rhymes. Because of this, few of his poems are sophisticated enough to achieve unity in both form and content, the hallmark characteristics of a successful poet's work. It is unfortunate that his dabbling in free and blank verse, which is much more amenable to his contemporary themes, makes up so little of his poetic output.

Hill's sporadic book publishing over the next thirty years was due to several factors: his growing law practice; his marriage to Mary Gladys Keith in 1933; his interest in camping, fishing, gardening, and traveling; his appointment as a police judge in 1942; and his obligations to a growing family that added two sons: David and Randy. Although he published no books in the 1930s and only one per decade during the 40s and 50s, he still managed to write poetry when he could find the time. Subsequently, he still placed poems in a wide variety of periodicals from *Oklahoma Today* and *The Christian Century* to *The Oregonian* and *Nature Magazine*. During this period, he not only held offices in regional literary societies but also attended regional writers' conferences, serving as President of The Poetry Society of

Oklahoma, as Vice-President of The Oklahoma Writers organization, and as Staff Poetry Panel judge at the Southwest Writers' Conference for three years. In addition, he won such poetry contests as The Elberta Clark Walker Nature Poetry Contest in 1941 (for "A Mountain Minstrelsy") and The Byliners Poetry Forum Contest in 1952 (for his poem "Bard for Bo-Peep").

Although Hill was 63 years old when Governor Bellmon appointed him as poet laureate in 1966, he was still spry enough to promote poetry to Oklahomans while tapping into the state's pioneer spirit. While Bellmon's appointment was politically motivated due to Hill's service as a lawyer and judge, he did appreciate Hill's 1965 book *Frontiers of Soonerland in Song and Story* where the poet celebrates, as he states in the foreward, "the indomitable spirit of the type of individuals who made the great Sooner state of Oklahoma what it is today, to inspire and exalt the spiritual nature that every individual has, on occasion, felt, and recognized as the highest and best moments of his or her own life [. . .] the author hopes his readers may visualize frontiers beyond our present physical bounds of Soonerland, and be proud of what lies ahead." Indeed, Hill followed his own advice and charted a new course as poet laureate with his 1968 book *From Country Lanes to Space Age Dawn*, which shows significant growth thematically that resulted from his fascination with the new frontier of space exploration. Late in his life, he became more attuned to contemporary American culture than many of his predecessors had.

After Hill's appointment as poet laureate ended in 1970, Governor Dewey Bartlett named him the state's second Poet Laureate Emeritus out of respect for his literary and legal work. During the 1970s, Hill resumed a quiet life in Wewoka until he passed away on December 22, 1980, at the age of 77, leaving behind his wife and sons. Today, some of Wewoka's citizens can still remember Hill sitting in his family's pew in the town's First Christian Church, his profile unmistakable because of the ear that had been bitten off in the 1920s during a brawl in the Wewoka oil fields. For those who do not remember his poetry, his missing ear, or his love for Oklahoma, his grave can be visited in Wewoka's Oakwood Cemetery.

Selected Bibliography

Primary Works

Hill, Rudolph N. "Bard for Bo-Peep." *Oklahoma Silver Jubilee Anthology*. s.l. : Poetry Society of Oklahoma, 1959. 73.

————. *Curtain Calls Before Curfew.* s.l. : s.n., 1962.

————. *From Country Lanes to Space Age Dawn.* San Antonio: Naylor, 1968.

————. *Frontiers of Soonerland in Song and Story.* Oklahoma City: Adman, 1965.

————. *Red Ship Wings: Poems.* Wewoka, OK: Lasiter, 1929.

————. "The Spell." *Contemporary American Poets: 1928.* Ed. Horace C. Baker. Boston: Stratford,

1928. 142.

————. *Star of Peace on Trail of Cibola.* San Antonio: Naylor, 1954.

————. *Westward Wind and 20th Century Singing Words: Poems.* s.l : s.n., 1959.

————. *Whipping-Tree and Wagon-Trails Farewell; America Forever: Poems.* s.l. : s.n., 1942.

Secondary Works

"Best Known Southwest Poets to Attend Writer's Conference." *Corpus Christi Caller-Times*, May 23, 1953, 5-E.

"Byliners Poetry Contest Winners are Announced." *Corpus Christi Caller-Times*, Mar. 16, 1952, 8-D.

Boren, Lyle H., and Dale Boren. "Hill, Rudolph N." *Who is Who in Oklahoma*. Guthrie: Co-operative, 1935, 223.

Marable, Mary Hays, and Elaine Boylan. "Rudolph Nelson Hill." *A Handbook of Oklahoma Writers.* Norman, OK: U of Oklahoma P, 1939. 61–63.

"Rudolph N. Hill," *Strangers to Us All: Lawyers and Poetry.* Accessed April 29, 2013. <http://myweb.wvnet.edu/~jelkins/lp-2001/hill_rudolph.html.>

Selected Poems by Rudolph N. Hill

First Words

Perhaps by Spring-wood's loveliness aroused,
(Like angel, firelight seen through cave-dim smoke)
While skinclad forms in family-circle drowsed;
Man's first strange words through tiresome silence broke
There must have been long dreams primordial man
Was forced, at first, to keep within his heart,
With no way to convey them other than
A pantomime of hands, or sudden start
Into peculiar, swaying sort of dance,
Until his lips brought forth exciting sounds
He put together, haltingly, by chance;
And then thought, words—as deer pursued by hounds!
Since then, what mind can estimate the reach
Man's voice has had through influential speech?

Old Santa Fe Trail

Over the roll and swash of the prairies,
Purple, and pearl, and pink in the dawn;
Pitching and riding immeasurable areas,
Into the sunset have Prairie-ships gone.

Over old wagon-trains, creaking and rumbling,
Dusty-brown canvas bellied and swayed.
Gold in the sunset, ox-teams went stumbling,
Bound for the west with the Overland Trade!

Day-dreams of treasure, sacked from old galleons,
High-pooped and stately, trod by a Don;
Night-dreams disturbed by neighing wild stallions,
Dark on a ridge, by red moonrise drawn.

Desert Square-Dancers

Dust-storms, rising across the desert
Here and there, seen afar,
Become square-dancers.
Though sometimes rough, they leave less hurt
Than frolics of Yaquis or Mexican lancers.

Bowlegged cowboys, mesquite-chaps wearing,
Circle all, swing about,
Into place falling,
To catch señoritas—bloomed yucca—staring;
And swing them about to the west wind's calling.

On Wolf Creek
(A Villanelle)

Below the rapids, Wolf Creek yet sings,
As clear as bells, a haunting woodland song,
Through which, always, the dim primeval rings.

I heard it first on gentle, sun-gilt wings
Of mountain-winds, what distance borne along
Below the rapids, Wolf Creek Falls yet sings.

On banks where evergreen with poplar clings,
Gaunt squaws plait bark for papoose cradle-thong,
Through which, always, the dim primeval rings.

At dawn, a crimson robe of color flings
Across the blue;—while like a distant gong—
Below the rapids, Wolf Creek Falls yet sings.

Sunset, behind Sheep Mountain, loses things
Down here, where drifting cool the shadows throng;
Through which, always, the dim primeval rings.

Would you have beauty strum your own heart-strings?
When everything, it seems, has gone dead wrong!
Below the rapids, Wolf Creek Falls yet sings,
Through which, always, the dim primeval rings.

Ancient School Appling

In the gentle upstirring
Of Eden-lost jewels
From the deep pool of thought-sleeplessness,
Men here heard, as through old orchards, whirring
Of wings, like birds, or lost seraph, seeking
Learning's sky-vaulted mansions,
Bringing to log-cabins talking
Among pioneer teachers
That high-soaring thought must have usefulness;
Some remembering from days they went barefoot walking
The dusty roads past schools with age creaking,
Bench-desks: logs, stanchions.

Food for thought, months amassing
Here until school opened,
Fall-breezes whispering creation's timelessness
Through windows that Johnny Appleseed, passing,
Might well have gazed, to forget forest enchantment
For one tree of knowledge.
Just to hear voices babbling,
Barely louder than brook-song,
From the age-mellowed, dog's eared text hornbooks,
Might have pleased more than all his hermit-life, appling
In wanderings that brought no true life advancement,
Or set roots for college.

Bard for Bo-Peep

A gentle, cool, trochaic breeze
Stirs through my tall iambic trees.
Dactyllic stars of Spring-soft bloom
Their lovely, light-toed dance resume.
And from the pool, where shadows play;
Spondee of thought turns lighter gray.
Although I tried all night to chime
My thoughts to anapestic rhyme;
I could not find one lamb to leap,
With me, across the bars of sleep.
But with the dawn's first rosy gleam;
Rhyme-tailed, they leap into my dream!

The Oil Fields

Under lights that flared forth
All the night, over prairies,
Over stretches of low hills and hollows;
Under lights that saw sights as hellish at nights
As the star flares of Champagne or Flanders
Came the Moloch of greed and excitement,
Came the quick-swelling boom of the oil-fields
To Wewoka, the Mecca of Seminoles,
To the profitless land of their Nation.
Like the boom of the cannon, but silenced
A few years before at Armistice,
Came the dull, rumbling roar of the oil trucks,
With trailers, like caissons, behind them.
Overnight, sprang up derricks and houses;
New towns were born in a fortnight
And people thronged in to earn money,
To follow the lure of the oil-fields;
Or for reasons unmentioned, and private,
Best-known to the persons who had them.
"Jake Joints," with rude fronts, began building,
Dance halls, rooming-houses, and brothels,
Unpainted, thrown up, or together
In ugly, un-workmanlike manner,
The thing wanted most by the owners
Being haste in immediate building,
And an ever-pervading, unrestful,
Though curious sense of things hidden,
For these, so the shrewdest of traders
Who had followed the oil-fields for decades,
Declared were the things that made money,
That brought in the gold for the drillers,
Rough-necks, rig-builders, and skinners.
Well-paid were the ones whom the companies
Employed as workmen or bosses;
And their lives could be bought for "big" money.
True it was that men of refinement,
Of courteous and gentlemanlike manner
Were sure to be found if one wanted,

But these went usually un-noticed,
Though some were the sons of oil magnates,
Engineers, probably too
From Princeton, or Harvard most likely,
Superintendents or paymasters also;
But the general "run" of the people,
And mass of "just-arrived" population
Was the muck of the scum of the earth,
Or the flotsam and jetsam of nations.
So it was that the oil-fields invaded
The land of the Seminole Nation,
And the derricks advanced on allotments
Of many a freedman and Indian,
Making rich those once poor,
But bringing as well tribulations
In the form of shrewd lawyers, or bankers,
Lease buyers, oil-scouts, and merchants,
One and all who craved wealth,
Anyway determined to have it.
Pioneers, old farmers, and settlers
Lost their heads in mad speculation.
Overnight men of wealth,
Or ruined both here and hereafter—
At least so it seemed,
For their dealings were swift and unscrupulous.
Yet, through all, there was joy;
There was fiddling, and drinking, and dancing,
Church-gatherings, and prayer-meetings even.
For those who would ease their heart-breakings
Could do so in wine, or repentance.
There were dens, here and there hell-houses,
Where dope-fiends lay drugged out of misery.
There were stills back up in the mountains.
"Blind Tigers" were built
Around doorways and corners,
And all kinds of "joints"
Where drinking or gambling might flourish;
And every twilight beheld a new troop

Of short-skirted, scarlet-faced women;
And with such things as these,
For a time, so it seemed,
There was little of law, or enforcement.
The crime waves began in every oil-town,
At village, or wayside, or junction.
As in war, men were killed,
Many, hi-jacked, or robbed and assaulted.
Drunken men beat their wives
When, at nights, they came in
Excited with liquor and passion.
Revilings and cursings were common.
So it was, the oil fields hummed all through the day,
With suppressed, laborious excitement
To flame out at night in crimes of abandon,
Like fires of gas wells,
Mostly smoke through the day
But at night fierce and awful to look on.

Machine Age

Behold how glorious becomes our age
As men, like ants, walk down the massive maw
Of subways, canyon-walls we pass in awe,
While looking up the towering heights that gauge
Too well the future's vast-dimensioned rage
Of superpowered, machinery-driven sway
Above all life—a Titan age, with gray,
Steel hives of men, who flit from cage to cage!
But there will always be some region fair,
Some vast, clean pleasure like the airman's flight;
The sunshine-gardens of the upper air,
The starlit, dream-fringed glory of the night.
And ever-precious memories will be there
Of God, the Master-Builder, King of Might!

Oklahoma Oil-Fields

Have you seen Oklahoma oil-fields?
Slender, tapering derricks,—
Busy with men like bees!
Tall, giant bee-hives.
Lonely on some rounded hill,
One beckons to another, domed afar,
The dusky minarets
Of motely sultan-millionaires,
Who throng to Worship
Here from near and far!

Have you seen Oklahoma oil-fields?
The earth's broad countenance,
Pimpled with great rocks,
Red from sun-exposure;
Lined with stream-beds,
Jack-oak and cedar-bearded!
Black, gleaming, greasy with oil
As the corpulent Creek Indian's
Seminole-freedman wife.
Heart-beat of earth is here.

Sonnet of the Plains

I saw the plains beneath a misty moon
Outspread from eastern to the western sky,
And silence moved, where cowboys used to lie,
Alone, from watch to watch, nor late, nor soon
But always right on time—no whistled tune,
No strange alarm, no sound beyond a sigh—
The wind, you say—perhaps, it shivered by.
Some spirit past, I mused, had to come to croon
Above the heavy grass, where those had slept
Who used to dream beneath the winking stars;
Who knew the saddle-pillow, and had crept
Through many dawns down by the wagon fire
And now it seems I too had surely stepped
Into the past to warm with cowboy sires.

Remembrance in Autumn

You are gone. Gold days are strangely still.
A still, blue haze glamors field and forest.
Grapes hang blue, and white fluff flies from thistle.
The sumac burns. Wild geese fly south,
And I hear the Bob-White's whistle.

I remember a night—one cool, like this—
And a sycamore by the shallows;
Under the glow of a southern moon,
A coon-dog's bay, and there below
We stood in the gold-flecked shadows.

You are gone. And the nights are ever long.
Ever long, and gray and colder;
But I think the dreams of your younger years
Have all come back, in quiet way,
To cuddle around my shoulder.

Fragment of Farewell

And who shall know the surge and swell
Beyond this body's beaten shell,
Beyond that Somewhere's foam of time
Wherein we wove our little rhyme?

1970-1977

LESLIE A. MCRILL

Of Scottish, Irish, and English descent, Leslie Anson McRill was born on November 8, 1886, in Williamsburg, Kansas, the third child and second son of merchant Calvin Whitfield McRill (originally from Ohio) and his wife, Amanda Viola Tapley (originally from Michigan). This small town in east-central Kansas was the center of McRill's young world, the place where he spent typical childhood and teenage years and where he first learned his love of languages, taking four years of Latin and two years of German before graduating from Williamsburg High School in 1904. Helping his older brother Albert edit the *Williamsburg Republican* as a teenager and spending the summer of 1903 writing for a neighboring town's newspaper also developed McRill's life-long love of writing, journalism, and printing, vocations he never abandoned in his 95 years of life.

Dedicated to his older brother almost to a fault, McRill moved to the community of Grand in southern Oklahoma Territory immediately after graduation to help Albert run that town's newspaper. After spending a few months at this endeavor, McRill moved two hundred miles west to Watonga, where he joined his parents, both of whom had moved to Oklahoma to be closer their children. Here, McRill continued in the newspaper business, working for former territory governor Thompson Benton Ferguson at *The Watonga Republican*. After a couple of years here, however, McRill again followed his brother, this time to Epworth University in Oklahoma City to study foreign languages.

Not one to waste time, McRill completed his studies in four years, matriculating in 1911 with an A.B. degree as well as an Oklahoma State Teacher's Certificate. Because of his stellar work and good reputation, he was named Professor of Modern Languages at Epworth that same year and moved to Guthrie when the university relocated there as the Methodist University of Oklahoma. One of his duties in this position required him to fill in as a minister at local churches. After several visits to a Methodist church in the town of Ripley, he became its official minister and ended up serving three separate terms there. Unknown to McRill at the time, this was the most stable period of his working life.

After living in Guthrie for eleven years, McRill relocated back to Oklahoma City in 1922 when the Methodist University of Oklahoma returned, this time as Oklahoma City College. Even though his parents now lived in OKC, McRill stayed for only one year, moving on to Los Angeles in 1923 to earn his master's degree in French at the University of Southern California. This move proved a pivotal one for the future poet. Although he held an advanced degree by the age of 40, he decided not to return to academe but spent most of the next fifteen years either back in the printing business or working as a secretary in his brother's law office. Being away from teaching, however, gave him time to focus on his writing, especially poetry. Ever the scholar, McRill became engrossed with Native American history and myth, reading more than 70 academic books and articles on the subjects. This decade-long engagement with writing and studying gave birth to McRill's first book of verse, *Tales of the Night Wind* (1945).

Mammoth by conventional poetry standards, *Tales of the Night Wind* includes over 120 of McRill's poems, serving as a compendium that collects the stories and legends of Native Americans by depicting their heroism, ceremonies, dances, medicinal practices, and religious beliefs in verse form. Using source material from several different tribes—from the Apache and Kiowa to the Cherokee and Mingo—McRill attempts to document their "life, struggles, beliefs, and [. . .] gradual adaptation to our life and customs." However, the last of these four objectives proves problematic, creating an ultimately flawed book. Like his predecessor to the poet laureate position, Rudolph N. Hill, McRill seems unaware of the irony of using antiquated European verse forms and a "white" scholarly lens to depict Native American life. In the book's preface, the poet illustrates his ignorance of such contradictions by privileging the dominant, Anglo point of view, stating that "history, for the most part white man's history, written for our purposes and with our own viewpoint, still gives the red man, in spite of the tales of bloodthirstiness, a position not inferior among the races of mankind." Although McRill's intentions were good, the people he yearned to depict positively often come off as anachronistic caricatures when placed within the confines of sonnet forms, hard rhymes, end-stopped lines, and European figurative language. The reality is that McRill lacked the skill to cypher Native American peoples and culture. Unfortunately, he fails to blend Native American and Anglo life coherently to present a realistic, syncretic view of both cultures, unlike his predecessor Anne R. Semple and his successor Maggie Culver Fry, both of whom succeeded due to their dual heritages. His repetitiveness in style and content tires the reader quickly, weakening the book's overall effect.

Although McRill had been working on what became *Tales of the Night Wind* for most of the 1930s, the book did not see publication until the end of World War II in 1945. Always full of vigor, McRill spent most of the war in Amarillo, servicing B-29 airplanes after he had been turned down as an enlistee. Even though he was almost 60 years old, the mid-1940s started the most active period of his literary career. Upon returning to Oklahoma City after the war, he became fully engaged with the area's thriving literary community by mentoring younger writers, self-publishing his own books, publishing and promoting books by others, and writing articles on Oklahoma for regional magazines and journals, especially *The Chronicles of Oklahoma*. He served one year as president of The Oklahoma State Writer's Association as well as eight years as the President of the Oklahoma Poetry Association. With this last organization, McRill also chaired the editing committee—on which sat former poet laureates Bess Truitt and Rudolph N. Hill—for the *Oklahoma Silver Jubilee Anthology* (1957), a book that celebrated Oklahoma's 50 years of statehood. Although he did not abandon work on Native American sources—in 1970 he self-published the verse play *Destruction of Awatobi: A Tragedy* —he found more appropriate poetic material later in life by writing about the state of Oklahoma and pressing contemporary issues. At the time he was appointed as Oklahoma's ninth poet laureate by

Governor Dewey Bartlett in 1970, he had just published *Living Heritage: Poems of Social Concern*, in which he discussed space exploration, the Vietnam War, civil rights, and computer dating. Halfway through the volume, he also translated a series of poems by such European writers as Victor Hugo, Théophile Gautier, Friederich Schiller, and Maeterlinck, putting his knowledge of foreign languages to good use. Despite being 84 years of age, the oldest poet laureate ever appointed, he remained mentally engaged with the topical world around him even though he was physically too old to treat the poet laureate position as more than ceremonial.

Although McRill remained Oklahoma's poet laureate until Maggie Culver Fry was appointed by Governor David Boren in 1977, he left the state in 1974 for Cincinnati, Ohio, following a young poet by the name of Dan Proctor whom he had mentored for several years. McRill's last book, *After-Thoughts in My Ninety-Fifth Year* (1982), was published the year he passed away. Serving as a "Selected Poems" with a brief biographical introduction, the volume contains examples of McRill's lifetime of poetic subjects: Native American history and myth, space exploration, Oklahoma's towns and characters, and the importance of religious contemplation. Although he died on March 8, 1982, in Cincinnati, McRill's heart always belonged to Oklahoma. After death, his body was shipped back to Oklahoma City for burial, putting "a beautiful close to a busy and fruitful life," a fitting quote he used to end the biographical section of his final book.

Selected Bibliography

Primary Works

McRill, Leslie A. *After-Thoughts in My Ninety-Fifth Year*. Cincinnati: Sn, 1982.

———. *Destruction of Awatobi: A Tragedy*. Oklahoma City: Leslie A. McRill, 1964.

———. "Ferdinandia: First White Settlement in Oklahoma." *Chronicles of Oklahoma* 41, no.2 (1963): 126–59.

———. *From Day to Day, As Seen Through My Binoculars*. Oklahoma City: Adman, 1972.

———. Gnomedal, Earth Spirits Dale," *Heavener Runes: A Poem*. Oklahoma City: Adman, 1967.

———. "The Heavener Enigma: A Rune Stone." *Chronicles of Oklahoma* 44, no.2 (1966): 122–29.

———. *Living Heritage: Poems of Social Concern*. Oklahoma City: Leslie A. McRill, 1970.

———. "Music in Oklahoma by the Billy McGinty Cowboy Band." *Chronicles of Oklahoma* 38, no. 1 (1960): 66–74.

———. "Old Ingalls, the Story of a Town that Would Not Die." *Chronicles of Oklahoma* 36, no. 4 (1958): 429–45.

———. "A Review of the De Soto Expedition in Territories of Our Present Southern United States." *Chronicles of Oklahoma* 39, no. 1 (1961): 70–79.

———. *Saga of Oklahoma: A Poem of Progress and Growth*. Sl: Leslie A. McRill, 1957.

———. "The Story of an Oklahoma Cowboy." *Chronicles of Oklahoma* 34, no. 4 (1956): 432–42.

———. *Tales of the Night Wind*. Oklahoma City: Dunn, 1945.

McRill, Leslie A., et al., eds. *Oklahoma Silver Jubilee Anthology*. Sl: Poetry Society of Oklahoma, 1959.

Secondary Works

Butler, Chris. "Poet and His Understudy: Age Gap no Barrier to Friendship." *Prescott Courier*, Jan. 11, 1979, 5.

"Leslie McRill." *Toledo Blade*, March 9, 1982, 17.

"Writer Dies at Age 95." *NewsOk*. March 9, 1982. Accessed May 6, 2013. <http://newsok.com/writer-dies-at-age-95/articles/1976328.>

Selected Poems by Leslie A. McRill:

Giants

On Pelion Mount Ossa's height they hurled
   When conflict raged in other far-off day;
   And Giants from the combat took their way
To distant corner of the Western World;
A new Olympus choosing, flags unfurled,
   Above its snowy heights they work and play
   And sing the weirdest melody, a lay
That broods through gloomy forest, rough and burled.

Sometime, e'en yet, the mighty mountains pop
   With anvil strokes, or evening's thickening dusk
In shivery dread upon the drooping pine
   Bears harmonies from their lofty top,
Where trumpet mastodons with gleaming tusk
   And fall to sharp commands in martial line.

(The Indians believed in a race of giants dwelling in Mount Olympus in the Northwest. Sometimes they saw them moving through the forest, breaking huge trees as they walked, or heard them singing weird, ear-splitting tunes.)

Logan's Speech
(Mingo)

Did e'er to Logan's cabin suppliant come
    Who left him, naked, hungry, or in cold?
    The white man's friend, the Mingo chieftain old,
Must now in anger turn, to grief succumb;

Deprived of loved one's, let his tongue be dumb
    And cease to praise, where once it was most bold
    To counsel peace and friendship; none doth hold
A drop of blood, his line to carry on.

But not in fear doth Logan hesitate;
His vengeance now is glutted in red blood.
The beams of peace he welcomes, yet alone
To him most dear, his country's fate;
He will not yield the place where he has stood,
Since none remain to mourn for Logan, gone.

Kicking Bird
(Ton-a-en-ko)

When warriors sat in chains with bold contempt,
    Defying all who dared to counsel peace,
    Old Kicking Bird they scorned, and bade him cease
To favor white man's law or ever tempt
The gods that rule, who never will exempt
    The red man from their will nor yet release
    Him from the rites, no matter where he flees;
They prayed a curse on Kicking Bird's attempt.
"Before the dawn bring forth fluorescent flame,
    Shall death hold rendezvous with scorned chief!"
Then Kicking Bird sat down to dine and smiled
    At threat of prisoners, chained; past his belief
That they could harm him with their ravings wild.
    E'er food had touched his lips the spectre came.

(Some said Kicking Bird was poisoned, others that it was a heart attack, but the old Indians said: "Our curse was on him." Mamanti, the Do-ha-te, Great Owl Prophet, declared he would hex Kicking Bird, although to do so meant that he, too, would die for it, as it was contrary to Great Spirit to hex a member of one's own tribe. Soon after, Mamanti also died.)

Burial

(Apache)

Down deep in yawning chasm,
    So far that no light of sun
May ever bring hint of twilight,
    And stillness blends into one
With black of the night's thick curtain,
    Keep vigil with splendid forms
Of pony, still war accoutered,
    And dogs, that defy the worms;
They lie there and wait the moment
    When out of the dark crypt's pall,
The Master's calm voice will summon
    To follow the battle call.

Near by in his regal blankets
    The chieftain sits, throned, apart;
The head-dress of gaudy feathers
    And paint splotch above the heart
Give sign of his mighty prowess,
    When over the rocks above,
He rode with the war cry sounding,
    And guided the skillful move
From stronghold to secret mesa,
    Then back to the heights again;
Stout heart, stouter still the mummy,
    And firm on its throne, the brain.

Evil's Snare

(Crow)

Old age is evil's snare—
    Naught lives for long but rocks;
Let young men nobly dare,
Since age is evil's snare;
But glory past compare
Is won in battle shocks;
Old age is evil's snare,
    And naught lives long but rocks.

Messiah

The message had come in its mystery wording,
　　Messiah's voice, waking in slumbering chord;
His coming was certain and dancers envisioned
　　The Prophet's return with the heartening word,
The white men had forced Him to lie in a manger,
　　They made for Him nothing of feasting or song;
They crucified Him on a tree with briars
　　Crowned noble brow's circle, unscarred by a wrong.

The red men placed tepee on high, pleasant mountain,
　　Within it they set the bright, shining, new bed;
Soft furs, rich and rare, for its downy reception
　　To Him who should come by their own prophet led.
And clothed in pure white with their priest's incantations,
　　And paint from the Prophet's far, beckoning shrine, —
The red as a symbol on check of the followers,
　　They sang as they prayed for Messiah's true sign.

The Medicine Man traveled far to the northward,
　　Crossed mountains of snow and wide rivers of ice,
Till there in a cabin he questioned the spirit
　　Who counselled but dimly and made sacrifice
To Great Spirit's leadings for life and its issues,
　　But naught knew he more than the prophet who came;
Discouraged, disheartened, he left for his homeland
　　And quenched in his heart the pure, faith-glowing flame.

In vain they had waited; in vain was their longing;
　　The white man still ruled and the buffalo, gone;
Hope died in their hearts, for their faith no rewarding;
　　The tepee stood silent on mountain of stone.
No guest for its welcome, Messiah had answered
　　Their prayers in a mystery they could not see—
No tepee may harbor the Presence that whispers
　　In heart of the red man: "Come, come unto me."

(The Indians reasoned that the white man had had the Messiah, and there was no reason why He should not come to them. They were going to see to it that He had a better reception from them.)

Eternal Purpose
(Echo)

With vibrant magic thrill
A thought comes from the ether wave—
Eternal Purpose.
Eternal Purpose
Still shapes the trend of earth's advance
With vibrant magic thrill.

"Boomer! Sooner!"

Oh, "On to Oklahoma!"—this the cry!
As hardy "Boomers" sounded reveille
To waken listless Nation, and defy
The force that bade them suffer more delay;
Prophetic eye that sensed the gala day
When far and wide each views his own demesne—
These "Sooners" marching on with Captain Payne!

Sod House

Though crudely built from Nature's own lent-sod,
You served mankind against the tempest's blast—
Wild winter-winds' swift flying hoofs unshod—
Your sturdy walls protected and held fast
A loving home for little feet that trod
The virgin prairies set with golden-rod.
O loved sod-house, sweet memories from your day
Stress evening hour when family knelt to pray!

In South Vietnam
Undeclared War of the 1960s

In South Vietnam our soldiers shoulder arms
And wade the swamps while snipers mow them down;
All this for Liberty
To free downtrodden man.
At least that's what the Pentagon proclaims
In daily press reports released for us.
But every mother's son
Who falls in murky swamp
May well be future generation's light—
A scientist, a president, a seer
The world has lost, and so
We wonder if the cost
Be justified in God's omniscient sight.

Reverie
(Summer 1963)

The black man is on the march . . .
That long, gaunt shadow etched in seething cloud seems strangely
familiar. It broods on the scene as
   in those sixties of long ago;
Its counterpart said: "This nation, half slave, half free . . . cannot
survive . . . a house divided against
    itself" . . .
"Glory, glory hallelujah" . . . . Voices stilled so long ago are heard again,
They ring down the hundred year corridor.
"We shall prevail!" the white-robed throng is singing . . .
The marching feet shake the pavements of Washington . . .
Simon Legree has loosed his hounds again!

Electric prodpoles push back marching men
And songs are dashing echoes from the frowning jailhouse walls.
A man stands in the school-house door!
The bellowing behemoth of Progress moves relentlessly on;
Brass-helmeted boys take up "the white man's burden" . . .
"Ye shall know the truth . . ."
That germ of Truth, proclaimed to march forever on . . .
And patiently He stands to Whom one day is as a thousand years.
The prophet cried, "How long oh Lord, how long?"
But man is feverish, impatient of the day.

The Potter alters once again the first conceived design . . .
New flaws have weakened human moulding clay . . .
Now He re-forms as best He may . . . The wheel turns on.
One hundred years the wheel is turning on since one who saw
          the vessel of his nation scarred upon
that cruel wheel of Fate . . .
Then some one reverently said:
    "Now he belongs to the Ages."
In our day the wheel still turns . . . .
But no one save the Potter knows the form and shape the
          clay is taking.

Old Homestead

SALUTE! Old Homestead, gaunt bleak wind-swept pile!
Deserted, yet you rear with pride your shaky frame,
But once a youth called you his home and while
He grew and toiled in cotton, trudged the weary mile
To country school to learn how man is set to tame
The universe and conquer distant spatial game,
Here sensed a vision of the great Creator's smile,
This youth who climbed each night your sturdy oaken stair
Or slid the bannister at early dawning hour,
Learned here the simple rules of Freedom's boon;
Built honesty and love for fellow man, a dare
To give for country all his manhood's ready power
And make for man a "giant step" upon the moon . . .

A Rondel

"A good listener is not only popular everywhere, but after a while he knows something." —*Watchman-Examiner*

Ears are not made to close, my dear friend;
Mouths, on the other hand, certainly are.
Listening often rewards one with par
And augurs some valuable goal at the end.

An ear that reception can carefully lend
Will beckon instruction from teachers afar;
Ears are not made to close, my good friend;
Mouths, on the other hand, certainly are.

To all eager minds the gods will soon lend
A message from some far-off glistening star,
But babbling mouths tend mostly to bar
Secrets that fortify souls and defend.
Ears are not made to close, my dear friend.

1977–1995

MAGGIE CULVER FRY

Maggie Culver Fry's Oklahoma ancestry runs deep. It can be
traced back to her maternal great-great-grandfather, Jacksquawn
Miller, who operated a stage coach stop outside of Vian in the
Cherokee Nation and to her maternal grandfather, George Deerskin
Waters, who traveled the Trail of Tears from Georgia into Indian
Territory and who later served as a member of the Cherokee Senate.
From her grandmother, Mary Catherine Miller Waters, who helped
Jacksquawn run the coach stop in Vian, Fry received her gifts of
music, storytelling, and spirituality, which were transmitted and
further perpetuated by her mother, Maggie Waters (affectionately
called Wintie). On July 11, 1899, at 17 years of age, Wintie married
Edward Culver, a white Muskogee resident from Mississippi who had
been gravely injured in the Spanish American War. Just over a year
later, on July 28, 1900, the couple's first child, Maggie Culver, was
born in Vian. Although the baby had the same given name as its
mother, this rarely caused confusion since the little one was
affectionately nicknamed "Sookie."

Because of his chest injury, which left a bullet lodged in his left
lung near his heart, Maggie's father was prone to bouts of sickness
that often affected his ability to work. For this reason, the Culver
family was often hard up economically during Maggie's childhood.
Although money was not plentiful, storytelling was. From her mother
and grandmother, she learned about Native American folklore,
regional history, and family stories in both English and Cherokee.

Even though Maggie never became fluent in Cherokee, she did immerse herself in the culture, deciding early on to document what she saw, heard, and experienced as an Oklahoman. Subsequently, she began writing poetry at the age of 12, starting her mother's belief that she would one day become a professional author, one who was "going to be something great," even though Maggie had her own doubts at the time.

Since her father was unable to work steadily, Maggie dropped out of high school at age 16 to help support the family. Despite working first as a salesclerk and then as a telephone operator, she educated herself at night by reading voraciously. Finally, at age 20, she returned to high school in Porum only to drop out again due to failing health caused by her strenuous work/study schedule. After this occurred, she moved to Verdigris, the town where her family had relocated. It was here at a church social that she met the love of her life, Merrit Fry, a fellow Cherokee who lived on a neighboring farm. They married in 1924. With Merrit's support, Maggie Culver Fry began seriously writing, composing the rhythm of her first poems on an old piano housed in her farm's chicken shack. Fry's only instruction came from a creative writing course at Tulsa University and other correspondence courses she took later.

Despite keeping busy with local agricultural and 4-H clubs, teaching Sunday school, raising two sons, and being a case worker for the Oklahoma Emergency Relief Administration, Fry's tenacity kept her working on her poetry for the next three decades. Her first nationally published poem, "Restless Angels," was turned down 73 times before finally finding a home in 1944. Her growth as a poet was slow, but steady. It wasn't until the early 1950s, after she and her husband had moved to Claremore, that Fry decided to put together a volume of her own work. As she stated in an interview with the *Tulsa World*, "I was digging potatoes in the garden when it came to me that I should write these things down." As she tells the story, God said to her, "little child, we're going to write a book."

Published in 1955, *The Witch Deer: Poems of the Oklahoma Indians*, contains verse relating Native American folklore, history, and their struggle to live in a harsh land. The book, however, also contains landscape poems, elegies, and religious poems, topics that Fry would explore throughout her professional writing career. Although *The Witch Deer* was privately published and ran only 40 pages in length, it received national attention, having been favorably reviewed in magazines and newspapers as far away as Syracuse, New York. It ended up selling 3,600 copies before the poet decided to stop its publication.

In spite this initial success, Fry continued to work at traditional day jobs. From 1955–65, she served as the personal secretary to Senator Clem McSpadden, a nephew of Will Rogers. Because she never learned to drive, she rode with him from Claremore to Oklahoma City and back, using the driving time to scribble verse on any available paper in the car. During this period, she also began focusing more on writing short fiction and essays about important Oklahoma figures, publishing in such places as *The American Mercury* and *Oklahoma Today*. Due to her busy work schedule, varied writing interests, and community service, it took Fry 16 years to put together her next book of poems, *The Umbilical Cord* (1971), which became an even greater success than *The Witch Deer*.

Although *The Umbilical Cord* explores the same themes as her first book, it shows much more growth and sophistication by illustrating the universality of local and regional experiences. As Fry discussed with interviewer Veima Nelbeltding, *The Umbilical Cord* has "a spiritual connection . . . The basic beginning . . . in that [the] umbilical cord draws me back to the source of the river, back where the loom keeps spinning and spinning." While Fry explores this idea in such poems as "Eternal" and "Transplanted," she also breaks new ground with "The Wheels Keep Turning," a long ecological poem that mourns the death of nature and poetry at the hands of technology and the incessant need for functionality. Additionally, in such elegies as "Shaft of Eros" and "First Love," Fry depicts the loss of love and its affect on the human spirit, another universal theme that readers easily related to.

Upon its publication, *The Umbilical Cord* was nominated for the Pulitzer Prize in poetry by a literature professor at the University of Chicago, making Fry a national literary figure. Her book, however, was beaten out by William S. Merwin's *The Carrier of Ladders*. Six years later, Fry earned another accolade when she was appointed as Oklahoma's tenth poet laureate by Governor David Boren, having been nominated by the Oklahoma Poetry Society. Early on in her 18-year tenure, Fry was active in the position, giving poetry readings, mentoring younger poets, visiting elementary and high school classrooms, and serving as Writer-in-Residence at Claremore Junior College. Despite her busy schedule, she also continued to write, publishing her third book of poetry, *Buckskin Hollow Reflections* (1978), in which she found new expression in prose poems and haikus; a children's book about Oklahoma humorist Will Rogers (1978); an autobiography entitled *Sunrise over Red Man's Land* (1981), in which she reminisces about her family life; and the historical *Cherokee Female Seminary Years: A Cherokee National Anthology* (1988). Even though she continued to write into her nineties, she was crippled with arthritis and was cared for in a nursing home after her husband Merrit passed away in 1991. When Fry was finally replaced as poet laureate by Carol Hamilton in 1995, she was named State Poet Laureate Emeritus out of respect for all she had done for poetry, literature, and Oklahoma.

By the time of her death on April 7, 1998, Maggie Culver Fry had been writing seriously for over 70 years, having published more than 800 articles, stories, and poems during her lifetime—a phenomenal feat for any writer. Today, she is one of the most esteemed of the Oklahoma Poets Laureate for her hard work, dedication to teaching children, and for her love of the state. As she writes in *Sunrise over Red Man's Land* "[. . .] when I hear the strains of 'Oklahoma, where the wind comes sweeping o'er the plain . . .' an overwhelming joy rises up within me . . . Oklahoma and I are one! We belong to each other." Today, fans can take solace in the fact that as long as Oklahoma exists, Maggie Culver Fry's work will be remembered.

Selected Bibliography

Primary Works

Fry, Maggie Culver. *A Boy Named Will: The Story of Young Will Rogers*. Sl: Bluestem, 1979.

———. *Buckskin Hollow Reflections*. Muskogee: The Five Civilized Tribes Museum, 1978.

———. *Cherokee Female Seminary Years: A Cherokee National Anthology*. Claremore: Rogers State College P, 1988.

———. "The Eternal Fire." *Oklahoma Today* 14, no. 1 (1963–64): 34–36.

———. "Five Day Picnic." *American Mercury*, Aug. 1960, 47–50.

———. "Memories of Lynn Riggs." *Oklahoma Today* 10, no. 1 (1959–1960): 32.

———. "Scientist." *Oklahoma Silver Jubilee Anthology*. Sl: Poetry Society of Oklahoma, 1959. 41.

———. *Sunrise over Red Man's Land*. Claremore: Claremore College P, 1981.

———. *The Umbilical Cord*. Muskogee: Oklahoma Printing Company: 1971.

———. *The Witch Deer: Poems of the Oklahoma Indians*. 1954. Claremore: Claremore Junior College, 1955.

Secondary Works

Bataille, Gretchen M., and Laurie Lisa, eds. "Fry, Maggie Culver (1900–1998)." *Native American Women: A Biographical Dictionary.* 2nd ed. New York: Routledge, 2001. 112.

Crawford, Bill. "State's New Poet Laureate Inspires Young Students." *Lawton Constitution,* Sept. 28, 1977, 11C.

Curtis, Gene. "Only in Oklahoma: Poet Laureate Started Writing at Age 10." *Tulsa World,* July 30,2007. Accessed June 5, 2013. <http://www.tulsaworld.com/site/printerfriendlystory.aspx?articleid=070730_1_A4_Poetl32238.>

Kay, Ernest, ed. *International Who's Who in Poetry.* 2nd ed. London: International Who's Who in Poetry, 1970.

Nelbeltding, Veima. "Interview with Maggie Culver Fry." May 15, 1973. Western History Collections, University of Oklahoma, Norman, OK.

"Poet Maggie Fry Dies." *Cherokee Messenger,* May 1998. Accessed June 5, 2013. <http://www.powersource.com/cherokee/message/0598.htm.>

"Woman Appointed State Poet Laureate." *Lawton Constitution,* July 23, 1977, 4A.

Selected Poems by Maggie Culver Fry

The Witch Deer

Marked like a fawn—and flecked with dark and light
As birchbark, splotched with shadows, soft and gray—
It was a wraithlike thing they talked about
Around the fire, after the hunting day.
"Witch Deer," they whispered, when a hunter skilled
Brought back this limp and bleeding beauty, killed.
Half phantom, theme of tales—they knew it meant
One thing alone—a change of government.

So breaking loose their bleeding tendrils, bare
Of Georgian soil, they started on from there . . . .
Theirs was a stony trail, a muddy sky;
The blizzard roared, the snowfall drifted high.
They crowded back the tide of unshed tears
And scooped out graves for loved ones; days like years
Seemed pulling down to trip their feeble grope,
Until one day they knew the joy of hope.
The wind grew kind, they heard the robin sing,
Wild onions grew, the dogwood burst . . . spring!

The red leaves fell, the skinned corn simmered on the fire;
The seasons passed, thanksgiving, heart's desire;
With sturdy homes and schools for girls and boys,
And worship every Sunday . . . many joys.

  *   *   *

Near old Park Hill one bracing sunny day,
A fretted patch of shadows seemed to sway . . .
Then wheeled to meet the singing bit of lead!
What was it . . . long ago . . . the sires had said?
"Witch Deer" . . . peculiar thing . . . few eyes would see . . .
A change of government.

  *   *   *

It came, the flag with stripes of red and white
And field of blue,
And stars, forty-five in all, and then a new
Was added to the flock . . . need I relate?
This WITCH DEER marked the dawning of a state.

The name "Witch Deer" was given to a deer of peculiar markings—quite rare.
The Cherokees believed that to kill one was to have a change in government.
Before the removal from Georgia, such a deer was killed, and after coming to
the Indian Territory, just before statehood, another was killed by Kale Starr at
Park Hill, Oklahoma. Again, the change in government followed.

Willow Wands

Across the Trail of Tears we carried willow wands;
Along the way we stuck them in the ground—
Another . . . and another . . . and another . . .
To mark our path; sometimes to mark the grave
Of one we loved . . . a sister or a brother.

Along the stony trail we left the willow wands;
Monuments alive, they whisper all
The frozen, choked-up heart could never say . . .
Weeping . . . stretching . . . like a wailing wall.

My husband's aunt Jane Wilkerson, who came to Oklahoma over the trail of tears, told of bringing willow wands with them. Where they stuck them in the ground along the way, they took root and grew.

Cradled

. . . And the Great Spirit said unto my mother,
"He is little, keep him warm . . .
Let his groping instinct feel
The thong-like sinews of my arm.
Keep him, at all times, near the voice of Love,
And keep his seeking eyes upon the sky."

And so she wove a cradle, and became my carriage,
And I never knew a fear!
Her pulsing warmth, her voice, her strength
Were near.

And now I am a brave;
You call me strong.
Lay every wreath of praise inside my cradle!
Give them to her, who taught me faith's bright song.

Indian Ball Game

Tarantelle, kaleidoscope of color,
Darting fast as feathered swifts and swallows,
Red man trades his solemn face for smiling
And sends his laughter rocking through the hollows.
Here a maiden leaps up like a falcon,
Brilliant skirt tail flashing in the sun,
Strikes the ball again, and sends it skyward,
Jubilant from games already won.
A handsome brave, his head bound in a turban
Of gay and multicolored calico,
Flashing smile and skin like gleaming copper,
Graceful as a bending willow bow.

Prairie Dearth

The little carcasses of prairie weeds,
Like standing human bodies, charred by fire . . .
Crisped to brittle hardness by the sun.
The rocklike slabs of sod divide and yawn
Until the cracks, like canyons, grow and grow.
The rushing stream is now a waterhole
With stamp of many hoofprints, where the mud
Is mauled to quivering softness, and its depth
Is brown and reeking muck . . . the only drink.
While straggling buffaloes, their ailing cows
Too lean to calve, lie down, instead, to die
Beneath the sun's sharp auger . . . the sky
That wan, blue socket, with a blazing eye!
And heat waves worm like spirit maggots, there
Above the earth they wriggle in midair.
In bitter pangs of feeble and dry birth,
As only stillborn hopes are clasped to earth.

Season in Travail

Another russet season
Choctaw bold,
is on its way.
Deep in the fevered groins
of summer, cicadas rasp,
clacking their rusty castanets,
they serenade the sick dry birth.
Incessant warring . . .
Warring against
their fated involvement
In one long
unbroken pain
of sound.

Cherokee Nation, Grantor

What romance in a deed to virgin land!
This one in my hand
Reads: "Cherokee Nation, Grantor"—before me,
Instead of this old document, I see
A waving, emerald sea of tall grass flowing
To meet the blue and bending rim of sky.

And then I see my town,
A miracle of rising walls where neon glows;
This one-time paradise for buffaloes.

The Wheels Keep Turning

MORNING.
In the distant asphalt meadow
I can hear the wheels.
Their purring is a snore,
Vibrating high above
All other sounds.
They are creeping in the sun
And they will never stop . . .
They <u>cannot</u> stop,
Until they have subdued
Green blades, and drowned
The tinkle of my brook.
The view of rolling meadows
Will be gone,
Replaced by silvered girders
And brick walls.
The wheels of concrete purpose
Were turning in the sun
Before that first sound backslap
At my birthing. And the wheels
From that first hot turning,
Like a golden vapor, in the deepest core
Of eternal purpose, at the dawn
Of day.
Abraham, with golden wheels
Turning him Canaanward;
The iron wheels of purposed faith
Matching the flashing glory
Turning within him.
The Pilgrims . . .
With hard wheels turning
As they crossed the sea;
Wheels of adamant resolve,
Their only chart.
And then, the wheels
Of pioneers,
Leaving a creamy wake
Of frontier dust.

MIDDAY.
The guttural, snoring sound
Of catapulting power
Is buzzing,
Hurting the very backbone
Of my life,
With hard, metallic vibration.
My noonday appetite is turned
Into a hard and hurting ball
Of revulsion.
It swells my belly.
I am a cow
Sick on poisoned cane,
On this, the last day
Of our lives.
The turning wheels
Have found us.
And our lovers tree
With roots embedded
Deep in dripping red
Of life,
Is shocked and torn.
It veers, a wounded ship
In a sea of churning gravel;
It goes down
Leaving a sick place
Where it used to be.
*   *   *

EVENING
We lie
In a frigid cubicle
With air-conditioned cold
Blowing
Through a spiraled hole
In the ceiling.
Lucky people, we!
The wheels have devoured, yet have left
A pocketful of gold.

We need not pick bright berries any more,
Or brighter dreams . . .
I had a window, once,
Where soft night air
Was sachet. Virginal scented
Moonflower. Now we have the cubicle
And cold and sterile air,
Coming from the spiral, overhead;
As cold and sterile as my dreams this night.
Oh let me store the capsule of what was!
Synthetic nutrient of the used-to-be,
Scented with jasper grass and violets.

I have grown barren; I cannot conceive,
And oh, my Darling, this our lover's kiss
Is not for sale, so much per column inch;
This is our privacy.

I dare not make the sacrifice
Of my last treasure; golden light
Crowning the very wheels of Breath . . .
I could not bear the raucous grate
Of pearls, ground in savage teeth,
Or see them stamped into the muck.

Was it this morning
I picked berries
And bright poems?
Tomorrow I shall walk
On a concrete field
And mourn my barrenness.

Far off down the road
I still can hear
The blunted snore
Of bulldoze power,
And blankly hear
The iron wheels roll on.

(By this time they have gained
Another hill).
"Poets," they say, "are fragile, sickly things
It takes such little things to make them die."
Meanwhile the wheels roll on . . .
As they have rolled
Since the day of that first hot turning,
As the wheels of flame
Turned within the deepest core of man
At dawning.

NEXT MORNING.
Today the golden halo
Casts a radiance
Over my memories, as I
Pick bright red berries
And brighter poems.
I know today, I have not lost my land,
For we are one . . .
And I shall ever carry with it within.
And now I know,
You cannot kill a poet or a poem!

Meanwhile, the wheels keep turning;
Only a few
Flower Children, try to outstrip them
On their way.

Far in the asphalt meadow
I can hear the wheels . . .

The Featherbed

My father lay, the shore receding from
His blue, and second-sighted eyes. He said,
"I never gave you much; I was not good
Or wise. I was a feathered cock with quills
to spare. Sometimes my feathers seemed as gold,
Because of you. This is the last black molt,
Today I lie, upon this feathered heap
With nothing save the memory of days."

I closed his lids, remembering his gift,
And truth denied, for he was good and wise.
I gathered up the feathers he had shed,
They made a cushioning, against the stones,
A sacrifice—a legacy to me.
A FEATHERBED, made from the strength he grew.

Eternal

The umbilical cord
Of my basic beginning,
Still draws me back
To the source of the river;
Where life from the loom
Keeps spinning and spinning . . .
No hand can undo
And no power can sever . . .
I am bound, I am bound . . .
To Forever, forever.

Transplanted

There was a mighty tree . . .
It branched and spiraled,
Bearing russet fruit
Above the lodge
Of old Echota.
Over the trail it came . . .
With mangled roots,
And for removed
From that warm soil
That nourishes
The core of trees.

The shocked fruit fell
Along the cheerless way,
Until at last,
Transplanted, thus to grow,
It thrust its roots far down
Into harsh clay
Of this new home.

Rains and snows
Have made a flowing balm . . .
A red clay salve
To heal the tentacles . . .
And bittersweet
Entwines the regal tree,
Which bears today
Resplendent fruit
For all the world
To see.

1995-1997

CAROL JEAN HAMILTON

When Carol Hamilton was named Oklahoma's eleventh poet laureate by Frank Keating in 1995, her selection did not come without controversy. Although the position had existed in the state for 72 years, most of the previous appointments had occurred at the whim of sitting governors. However, Law 25-98.4 changed that irregular practice in 1995. It called for a new poet laureate to be named every two years by the current governor from recommendations made by the state's literary societies and arts councils. Although the law was good in helping to define the role of the state's laureate, its source was questionable since the legislation was sponsored by a representative who had a constituent in Oklahoma City that actively sought the position. Even though nepotism was responsible for many poet laureate appointments, it backfired in this case. The woman who originated the legislation was never named to the position. The first casualty of her selfishness and self-interest, however, was Maggie Culver Fry.

Although Fry had served as poet laureate for 18 years, there were many who wrote to Governor Keating informing him that Oklahoma did not need a new poet laureate. In response, he asked that a committee be formed to find the most worthy candidates to replace Fry. After deliberations, at least two names were put forth: Norman Russell (Vice President of the University of Central Oklahoma) and schoolteacher Carol Hamilton. With virtually no fanfare, Hamilton won out, quietly receiving a certificate in the mail. As she relates, there was

> no letter of explanation, no calls . . . no nothing! I really had no idea if I were Poet Laureate or a finalist. It was quite some time before I was sure [. . .] There had not been a tradition of special projects for the post, and there was certainly no job description. I was asked to write some poems for special occasions: the National Endowment for the Humanities [. . .] in Oklahoma City and the opening of the Greenwood Center in Tulsa. I visited lots of schools, etc., but I already had been doing that.

One of her first acts was to enlist help from the Poetry Society of Oklahoma to name Maggie Culver Fry as Poet Laureate Emeritus. While Hamilton was definitely qualified to serve for the excellence of her poetry—especially since she won the Oklahoma Book Award in 1992 for her chapbook *Once the Dust* (1991)—the grace she showed in supporting Fry added a note of dignity to her tenure as well.

Most certainly, the poet learned such empathy from her parents: Clarence DeWitt Barber (an electrical engineer) and Ruby Settles Barber (an English teacher). Although both were native Kansans, they lived in Chicago and Kansas City before moving to Enid, Oklahoma, where their daughter Carol Jean Barber arrived on Aug. 23, 1935. When Carol was a teenager, the family pulled up stakes again, however, moving south to Midwest City, where they finally settled. Here, Clarence worked for Oklahoma Gas and Electric (OG&E), Ruby headed Midwest City High School's English Department, and Carol attended school, graduating in 1953. Unlike many young women at the time, Carol also attended college, earning a Bachelor of Science degree in Elementary Education from Enid's Phillips University in 1956, the same year she wed future legislator J. Jefferson Hamilton. They ended up having three children: Debra, Christopher, and Stephen.

After marrying, the couple traveled extensively, living in Scotland, Connecticut, New York, West Virginia, Ohio, and Indiana. Although she began writing as a child—scary stories were her specialty—Hamilton began professionally publishing articles and stories in national magazines while living in West Virginia and Ohio, the first of which "Winnie the Pooh as Existentialist" appeared in 1965. In the Ohio, she also met a friend who wrote poetry therapeutically and suggested that Hamilton do the same. She did. Surprisingly, the new poet found immediate publishing success and began giving public readings. Upon her return to Oklahoma in 1971, she made poetry an important part of her classroom. Further success came when her students at Tinker Elementary on Tinker Air Force Base won first and second places in Oklahoma's State Youth Poetry Contest. Upon taking them to receive their awards at the Contemporary Arts Foundation, she met current poet laureate Leslie McRill. Later, she met Maggie Culver Fry at the same event.

Although she has published a dozen poetry books since 1978, has won several awards, and has taught English at Rose State College and at the University of Central Oklahoma, Hamilton claims that

> I do not think I have ever had anything I wanted to accomplish with poetry. I had never had any interest in it at all until I began to write it, and then began the long quest to find poets I liked to read . . . .before that the only poet I'd ever really been drawn to was John Donne . . . .and some of the lyrics of the time by Dylan, Joan Baez, Simon and Garfunkel, and Judy Collins. The art is something with no end in sight for the learning curve, which is part of the attraction.

Partly because of these ambivalent feelings, Hamilton often composes thematic books of poetry with specific topics: *Breaking Bread, Breaking Silence* (2000) focuses on food; *Shots On* (2008) portrays female photographers and their pictures; *Contrapuntal* (2009) depicts the relationship between Clara Schumann, Robert Schumann, and Johannes Brahms; *Umberto Eco Lost His Gun* (2010) explores the effects of war on women, children, teachers, and artists; and *Lexicography* (2011) plays with words and the process of naming. No two books of hers are alike, which makes Hamilton one of the most eclectic of all the Oklahoma poets laureate. Surely, what fellow poet Ken Hada wrote about *Contrapuntal* is true of all her work: "Hamilton's poetic interpretation engenders understanding and empathy," creating readers who are "sympathetic, fellow travelers." No doubt, Hamilton's caring personality and playful creativity is what resonates most with her audience. Her debt to the metaphysical poets gives her poetry a depth and sophistication that many of her predecessors' work lacks.

Despite her talent as a poet, it seems that her appointment to the poet laureate position in 1995 (and her retirement from public school teaching in 1993) was the impetus Hamilton needed to start focusing more on writing poetry. Especially important was her reaction to the Oklahoma City bombing of the Alfred P. Murrah Federal Building on April 19, 1995. Taking her role as poet laureate seriously, she composed "Braced Against the Wind"—her most anthologized poem —just days after the event, expressing Oklahoma's history of strength and tenacity in the face of hardship. This event led her to believe that there is "a need for more of the kind of public poetry that we Americans so rarely write [. . .] public poetry has other layers of responsibility than most of our poetry has." Hence, instead of just offering lip service to survivors, Hamilton spent months helping them cope with their ordeal through poetry therapy, showing how integral Oklahoma's laureate is in times of crisis. Although Hamilton had published only three poetry books by the time of her commission, since the bombing she has published more than eight, making her elderly years the most prolific and productive of her life.

Continuing her dedication to Oklahoma after completing her tenure, Hamilton helped establish "The Woody Guthrie Poets" in 2004, which sponsors an annual poetry reading at the July Woodyfest in Okemah. At 80 years old, she still maintains an active lifestyle in Midwest City, showing no signs of slowing down. She rises at five o'clock every morning to write, composes a poem each day, translates Spanish for an Oklahoma City health clinic for women and children, and gives readings across the state. Even at this age, she still finds poetry exciting and intriguing: "the involvement of sound and the playing with words and the amazing moment when you are saying something you had no idea you were going to say all keep the process vital. I can't imagine thinking I had figured it all out." For such engagement, she was also recently named Poet Laureate for the 50th anniversary of Midwest City and Tinker Air Force Base. Such engagement should keep Carol Hamilton writing poems and serving her community for years to come.

Selected Bibliography

Primary Works

Hamilton, Carol. *Contrapuntal*. Georgetown, KY: Finishing Line, 2009.

———. *Daring the Wind*. 1984. Edmond, OK: Broncho, 1994.

———. *Desert, Dry Places, and Other Aridities*. Edmond, OK: University of Central Oklahoma, 1978.

———. *Gold: Greatest Hits* 1968–2000. Columbus, OH: Pudding House, 2000.

———. *I, People of the Llano*. Chonburi, Thailand: Good Samaritan, 2010.

———. *Legerdemain*. Los Angeles: Good Samaritan, 2000.

———. *Lexicography*. Greensboro, NC: March Street, 2011.

———. *Master of Theater:* Peter the Great. Georgetown, KY: Finishing Line, 2011.

———. *Once the Dust*. Edmond, OK: Broncho, 1991.

———. *Shots On*. Georgetown, KY: Finishing Line, 2008.

———. *Umberto Eco Lost His Gun*. Columbus, OH: Pudding House, 2010.

———. *The Vanishing Point*. Charlotte, NC: Mainstreet Rag, 2004.

Secondary Works

"Carol Hamilton." Accessed June 17, 2013. <http://www.carolhamilton.org/>.

"Enid Celebrity: Carol Hamilton." *EnidBuzz.com*. Accessed June 17, 2013. <http://enidbuzz.com/carol-hamilton/>.

Hada, Ken. "Contrapuntal." Review of *Contrapuntal* by Carol Hamilton. Visual Arts Collective Poetry. Accessed June 17, 2013. <http://vacpoetry.org/2009/09/29/contrapuntal/>.

Hamilton, Carol. Email message to author. June 19, 2013.

"Hamilton, Carol (Jean Barber) (1935–)." *Contemporary Authors*. Farmington Hills, MI: Thomson Gale, 2002.

Two Master Poets, Carole Hamilton, Oklahoma Poet Laureate, 1995–1997 [and] Carl Sennhenn, Oklahoma Poet Laureate, 2001–2003: A Centennial Tribute. Dir. Maggie Abel and Charles Maupin. Magster TV, 2007. DVD.

Selected Poems by Carol Hamilton

Flatland

I.
The barns are checkered
with sun setting beneath
clouds. Miles and miles
stretch punctuated by
triangles of western
light, pyramid-shapes
clarifying the landscape.
Grain elevators call
out where communities
lie and straight roads
skirt quarter sections,
lead clear to each
almost extinct town.
You can point them out,
name them from the road
signs, five or six
in a moment.

Nomenclature of families,
memories (phantoms
oddly extant somewhere
else), girls (or maybe
women, wives, or daughters,
mothers), pass by in
a hurry. Helena. Carmen.
Ingersoll. Aline. Goultry.
Amorita. Isabella. Sharon.

Furrows are as straight
as pride can make them.
My passing eyes dizzy
at the regularity.
Hopeful clans have
left remnants. Lovedale.

Freedom. Loyal.
Brace. Mutual.
Round-topped barns
of corrugated tin
spring up like
distant mountains.

A happy stirring
remembers something
from childhood.
Arrivals must have
Meant joy, though
I remember dour faces,
shy children, hard
work roughening
the handshakes.
Hugs were not facile
in that country. I
remember no effete
citified affection.
To be teased with
a nasal drawl and
a lop-sided grin
was welcome. There
I was mocked
and secure. Now
I feel lifted at
the timbre of voices
in the reverberating
metal cavern, surrounded
by hay lofts and
water troughs and
the spin of windmill.

Light beamed
back and forth across
the flattened black
of wartime sky.

I lay by a west window
and watched it,
feared bombers.
The light pinpointed
the prisoner-of-war
camp, searched me
out with questions.
Those strange enemies
could see as far
as I, could learn
names that meant
what they said.
Plain View. Sand Fork.
Red Rock. Stillwater.
Lookout. Pond Creek.
Driftwood. Ft. Supply.

Last summer she walked
onto the garbage pile
burning there, thought
of the creditors, and
died as another bit
of refuse. Humac and
Taloga looked on.
Waynoka and Burlington
stood by. Canadian
winds sang with snow.
The Rockies swept
down ice. The desert
blew up its dessication.
She watched the heat
waves curl around her.
Buffalo. Cimarron. Waukomis.
Jet. Ingersoll. Cherokee.
Wakita. They survive.
You can see far here.

Once the dust packed up
and went wandering.
We could not see
our feet between here
and there. Questions
were asked before.
Now names are etched
on the memorial.
They clatter with
consonants and keep
their connotations.
When there are no
blizzards or dust bowls
blinding, you can
see far. Very far.

    II.
That civilization of
triangles and chambered
death buried its
wealth and continued for
four thousand years
without a prairie,
with only a fertile valley.
Then even nomadic tribes
found resources for
future generations,
left stone tablets and
stories with beginnings,
middles and ends.
I see no resting
place on the horizon
and stories take up
mid-sentence, are left
dangling. It all erodes
and blows away until
the county agent passes
along the latest findings

from the university
experimental station.
Then the commodities
market staggers and
newscasters "tsk-tsk."
The people gather here
in booths at Love stations
or in state park campgrounds,
those surprising oases
come upon in fertile pools
below horizons.
Their voices are soft.
The language twangs
in a stately adagio
movement. But the
symphony only tours
through school gymnasiums.
And what they talk of
is futures and each other.

Then I knew we were
there because in
the distance was a
measured row of
trees, immature
but determined.

Now those trees
are grown, look
almost natural,
except they only
outline things.
They trace highways,
the road to the house,
a gulley which
carries moisture.
They too are landmarks.

The old man sat in
his swivel chair,
passed the hours
by the cooler with
chilled soda pops
and popsicles, among
crackers and tinned
soup and fossils
and dust and the past.
"The old chief," he
said, "used to be
in that glass case,"
he said, "and they took
him away," he said.
And his shop window
was cluttered but
empty of those
bones and best
fossils taken away
by the museum people.
He told us tales
and told us his losses
and soon after he
died and became
bones himself, having
passed over a century
telling of fossils
and bones found
and lost in that
dry land and of
waves of people who
came and left with
discoveries and
markets. Pictographs
and petroglyphs and
dinosaur tracks are
scattered everywhere.

The locals will
take you across dusty
fields. There is
no formal legacy.
You must search out
the stories and the
traces of those
who have been there.
The old chief
was lamented by his
caretaker, and now
he is packed away
in the storage rooms
of the university museum.

The old man is packed
away, too. There are
no monuments. There
are ruins, writings,
spaces shifting,
twitching, shrugging
us off. Coronado's men
scratched graffiti
as they crossed the land.
We pass over like crop
dusters. We move on
like cloud shadows. They
looked for Seven Cities
of Gold. Cibola is a
mirage, vanishes before
us like our images as
we walk into ourselves.
You can see far here.
Very far.

Face of War

Toni Frizzell followed
the battlefields of World War II,
a target, she said,
like a wooden duck
in the carnival shooting gallery.
The little boy come home
from play in London,
well-bundled in too-big clothes,
stares at us from the rubble
and tomb of his home,
his parents, his brother,
his life. He stares at us
forever. All her dangers
brings us home, too,
on our doorstep the moment after
some magician has pointed
his wand and, Poof!
Everything is gone.

Lambs to Lions

In Italy, he said,
they dressed the babies
in black to look like
Il Duce, called
the children toy soldiers.
First Gulf War, and
last week my 5th graders
had never heard
of Saddam Hussein,
now voted to make
their piñata
into his head,
beat him to pieces,
a pulp of papier-mâché
and candy to rain down.
Easily as dandelion heads
drifting off in white profusion,
we cultivate the children
with our unchecked dreams.

Tealeaves for an Undesignated Reader

The construction crew girl said
she had to write her poem on sheetrock,
no paper handy.
It was a little love verse,
unexceptional in every way.
When the ravine behind my Ohio house
hatched new snakes and the hillside
writhed with a race to survival,
when the shells, all perfect amalgams
of calcite crystal and keratin fiber,
broke open, each sounded
an alarm if I had been listening.
We leave tracks as we pass.
Graphite on gypsum or broken fragments,
slithers through mud,
some slight alteration to a planet already atilt with its past.

Cain's Ballroom

Oasis of the past hidden
In a labyrinth of overpasses
And one-way streets,

The dark sweatbox throbs
With over-amped music
And garish neon.

The bar flashes and jangles
While voices try to out-shout
The music. And the music

Is a cheerful juggler gone
Berserk or put on high speed
While telling tales of tragedy.

Moon Mullican, Red Foley
Look down from browning
Portraits. Roy Rogers and

Kay Starr are still young.
Leon McAuliff, Jimmy Wakely,
Bob Wills and the Texas Playboys

Are waxing crescents
Over the hot-breathed plains
On a summer night.

Gene Autry is now
My hero and not yet
A sausage in the saddle.

He pats Champion's nose
While we skim the slick
Dance floor and touch

With greasy fingers
From the barbecue.
"Get up and feed your chickens,

Before they raise the dickens"
Is 7:00 A.M. on the radio.
Cold morning. Gene and

Champion. Saturday afternoon.
Outside now, traffic thunders overhead
And air-conditioning boxes in.

Cain's creates welcomes makes is.
Here we are slick with sweat,
Relieved of too much comfort.

Their Love: The Schumanns

Their joy together was a nearly perfect thing,
Though Robert would have kept her as his own,
A hausfrau with extraordinary gifts to bring.

Her playing might, only at home, lilt and sing
For all their children and friends, the household known.
Their joy proved not quite a perfect thing.

Clara found her need of crowds and traveling
Was all too strong to stay a fully blown
Hausfrau, even with extraordinary gifts to bring.

When Schumann, frenzied, worked composing,
Clara could not practice, had to wait, postpone
Her art, their joy not quite a perfect thing.

Child on child was carried, birthed, given wing,
Then Robert's mad genius thrown into river like a stone,
This hausfrau must earn, her extraordinary gifts to bring.

She had to play and plan for all and also cling
To memories of how they loved and thought as one.
Their joy together, lost, a nearly perfect thing
To this hausfrau with extraordinary gifts to bring.

Creation

One author didn't note his daughter's birth
in his daily diary. And Joseph Conrad
wrote as his child lay dying.
Some think genius demands a Cyclops' eye,
bulging, bloodshot, never looking right
nor left, no tender gazes lingering.
Take a Berryman dragged behind his muse
like rags and tin cans behind a bridal car
speeding away to bliss. Yet Maugham told
of the painter, a woman possessed, her work
as bad as her dedication was pure.
Vehicles stuck in 5th gear.
Sometimes we're no use,
can't do the shopping stops,
can only make a dash for it
or break down at the side of the road.

Here is a quiet
Oriental page
where my eye rests
on brushstokes
scant print
ample space
Balance stills
     this frenzy.

Pushing Past the Labor Room

Give or take thirteen, fourteen years
and birth pangs take on fresh insistence
as you struggle for life
beyond the womb of care;
and no one instructs me in breathing now
nor tells me when to bear down,
when to relax.
There is no anesthetic.
And I remember the simple necessity
of direction, then,
the hovering, wondrous concern
all around. Where do I push,
if I push at all?
I think you do the pushing now,
wheeling me down the hall.

Braced Against the Wind

Nothing gentles down from
A mild Heaven here.
We are always braced
Against the wild wind.
We were ever hand in hand
As far as the eye can see.

Cataclysms are the story.
Our cities sprang up overnight,
Are flattened at a tongue-lashing
By clouds and bush-whackers, and
Bonnies and Clydes
Struck fast and hid against
The land stretched and pegged
Flat to the Four Corners
Of the Earth. We do not cower
At disaster.

We join hands, sing hymns.
We share tears and
Bend our backs raising
A neighbor's barn.
Do not think your
Abrupt terror will
Destroy us.

Wide horizons stretch our
Vision. We do not believe in limits.
We shift with the red dust,
Dance golden like the wheatfields.
We believe. We move on.
We bend and dance
On the tall grass.

The prairie sings our pain.
The land shouts our praise.
The wind calls us together.

1997–1998

BETTY LOU SHIPLEY

Betty Shipley's biography is one of the most ironic and tragic of all the Oklahoma poets laureate. Although she was commissioned by Governor Frank Keating as the state's twelfth laureate in 1997, she was the first to have both parents born in Oklahoma/Oklahoma Territory. Her father, Clay Henry Forsythe, was a telephone man who hailed from Deep Fork in Oklahoma County and her mother, Odessa Luella Lindesmith, was born in the town of Hennepin in Carter County. Even though Shipley's appointment came well after the advent of the internet and electronic publishing, less is known about her life publicly than many of her predecessors.

What is known, however, is that Betty Lou Forsythe was born in Edmond, Oklahoma, on July 11, 1931. As a child, she moved with her family (which also included brothers James and Dale) to Enid and then to Duncan, where she graduated from high school in 1949. Although her father used Duncan as a home base, he traveled around much of Oklahoma helping to put up telephone lines to the state's citizens for Southwestern Bell Telephone Company. Betty often went with him, learning a lot about the state and its people while still a child. Unfortunately, her parents passed away from cancer within six weeks of each other during the spring of 1950, her father at Easter and her mother during Mother's Day. Both were young: Clay was forty eight and Odessa forty one. Thus, Betty was left parentless at age 19. Shaken by this loss of family and security but sustained by her faith and spunky nature, she began working for Southwestern Bell and married oil field worker Bill Shipley a year and a half later in October 1951. The couple settled in Edmond, raising two sons—Billy and James—until her husband was killed in an automobile accident in 1959. Realizing that she had two children to provide for with a third, Kathryn, on the way, Betty decided to return to school in order to make a better life for her growing family. She enrolled in Central State University (now known as the University of Central Oklahoma) to earn a degree in secondary education.

After graduating, Shipley found herself in a variety of teaching jobs, all of which lent her the diverse experiences needed to become an award-winning teacher. Later, these experiences would inform her poetry as well. Her jobs included teaching workers in a factory, teaching at a Catholic school, being one of few white teachers at Douglass High School in Oklahoma City during the era of desegregation, and teaching at a school for pregnant teenage girls. However, Shipley eventually found a steady job teaching English at Edmond Middle School. It was while here that she received Edmond's Teacher of the Year award. Typical of her humorous nature, she had a photograph taken of her with the trophy standing on top of her head. Even though she saw teaching and writing as important, she always remembered never to take herself too seriously even though she was engaged in confronting social and political issues in her verse.

Like her immediate predecessor to the poet laureate position, Carol Hamilton, Shipley began writing poetry late. It wasn't until the 1970s that she began composing verse in earnest. This led her to earn a master's degree in Creative Studies from the University of Central Oklahoma (UCO). After she retired from the Edmond Public School system in 1992, Shipley devoted herself to writing poetry full time. She was also tireless in promoting the work of other contemporary poets both within and outside of the state.

Although Shipley had been writing for years, she did not give her first public reading until 1978 at the Norman Public Library, the same year she was appointed as Artist-in-Residence to Oklahoma schools. Her first book, *Called Up Yonder: Poems from the Bible Belt*, came two years later in 1980. As stated on the cover, the book contained sixteen narrative poems that depicted "death and dying in Oklahoma." Instead of being overtly morbid, Shipley undercuts the poems with black humor that lightens the mood, a result of her adult ambivalence toward the rituals of religion. As this volume illustrates, using humor to create catharsis is her greatest poetical gift. She endears readers by being funny, allowing them to confront their fears through laughter.

During this period, Shipley was also collecting and editing poems with Nina Langley for Full Count Press, the publishing venture that Shipley had started in Edmond. One of their books was the anthology *Meltdown: Poems from the Core*, which presented poetry about the nuclear age by such writers as Joe Bruchac, Karen Strope, and William Pitt Root. As Shipley and Langley state in their dedication (which alludes to T. S. Eliot's *Waste Land* and Ezra Pound's *Cantos*):

> This book is a reflection of the response many poets and other artists are having to the world in which they find themselves, a world of power and progress, poisoned lakes and rivers, air turned black with smoke and fumes. If the progress continues, the oceans will be dead in a decade or so in a world where a generation of people have strontium 90 in their bodies, asbestos in their lungs and DDT in their fat. That's the whimper.
>
> Then there's the bang: We may be close to the finish line of the nuclear armament race. Even now a blunt finger is poised over a red button which, if pushed, will engulf us in a nuclear firestorm, a disaster of mythic proportions. In the midst of all this, it requires an enormous amount of convolution for a poet to sit around and write about rainbows, and it is inevitable that our love songs sometimes become contaminated.

While the editors' statement may sound fanatical to contemporary readers, its underlying philosophy represents a cynical era in American history—epitomized by Pennsylvania's Three Mile Island accident, the No Nukes concerts, the Soviet Union's invasion of Afghanistan, and Hal Lindsey's predictions of Armageddon—where the average citizen worried daily about such dangers as synthetic poisoning, nuclear annihilation, and a dying environment. Today, *Meltdown: Poems from the Core* is important as an historical document, a fin de siècle tome that expresses America's lack of optimism and general malaise at the end of Jimmy Carter's presidential administration. It also shows that Shipley was one of Oklahoma's first poets laureate to be actively engaged with pressing political and social issues. Although she was self-effacing, this did not stop her from trying to make a better world for future generations.

Despite her burst of creativity during the late 1970s, Shipley did not publish her next (and final) book of poetry, *Somebody Say Amen*, until 1997. In the meantime, she continued championing other poets by operating Full Count Press and its replacement Broncho Press. With the latter, she published Carol Hamilton's *Once the Dust*, the winner of the Oklahoma Book Award in 1992. With this press, she also published work by Catron Grieves, Lance Henson, and Sandra Soli (whose book *Silvering the Flute* was runner-up for the Oklahoma Book Award in poetry). Young writers were especially appreciative of Shipley's rejection letters. Even though many of her letters denied publication, Shipley always let authors down easily and encouraged them to keep writing, giving them specific things to work on and improve. While running Broncho Press, she also served as poetry editor and columnist for *Byline* poetry magazine and taught in UCO's Creative Studies Department. Her own poems appeared in such journals as *Timbercreek Review*, *Phoenix,* and *Nimrod.*

Although *Somebody Say Amen* (1997) begins hopefully with Whitmanesque images of rebirth in "Spring Poem" and "Things are Spiffing Up," Shipley soon undercuts this positivity by writing more poems about death, dying, and the things one leaves behind, situations that haunted her throughout life. While these themes are the same as her first book's, *Somebody Say Amen* shows much technical growth by presenting clear images, emphatic parallelism, and longer narrative lines. She writes in a modern free-verse style with no regular meter or contrite rhyme schemes. Shipley's relatable style developed from her belief that "there's no profit to me in being obscure. It's unfair. You're supposed to be communicating here." Her uncanny wit is also still present in such poems as "Things Go Wrong" and "Because in the Context of Transition Someone in my Poetry Class Asked If I Really Would Like to Meet Jesus—Now." Due to her growth in skill, *Somebody Say Amen* was awarded the Oklahoma Book Award for poetry in 1997. Unfortunately, Shipley was unable to attend the awards ceremony and passed away from cancer on the night of the event: March 14, 1998. She was 66 years old. Her friend and publisher, Marcia Preston, accepted the award on her behalf.

Because of everything that happened to Shipley during her lifetime, readers can understand why she seemed obsessed with death and loss in her verse. The ending lines of her poem "What We Need" could serve as an appropriate epitaph: "[. . .] life is painfully beautiful / and only a few go mad." This sentiment is representative of both her life and work, as she must have surely known.

Selected Bibliography

Primary Works

Shipley, Betty. *Called Up Yonder: Poems from the Bible Belt*. Tulsa: Cardinal, 1980.

———. *Somebody Say 'Amen'*. Edmond: By-Line, 1997. Shipley, Betty, and Nina Langley, eds.

———. *Meltdown: Poems from the Core*. Edmond: Full Count, 1980.

Secondary Works

"1998 Oklahoma Book Award Winners." *Oklahoma Center for the Book*. Accessed June 19, 2013. http://www.odl.state.ok.us/ocb/98win.htm.

"Betty Forsythe Shipley." *NewsOK*. March 17, 1998. http://newsok.com/betty-forsythe-shipley/article/2606301. Accessed June 26, 2013.

"Oklahoma." *Poetry_About: The Noisiest Poetry Newsletter in the Known World*. Accessed June 19, 2013. http://groups.yahoo.com/group/poetry_about/messages/15.

"State Poet Laureate to be Remembered." *NewsOK*. Oct. 28, 1998. http://newsok.com/state-poet-laureate-to-be-remembered/article/2631059. Accessed June 19, 2013.

"State's Poet Laureate Dies." *NewsOK*. March 17, 1998. http://newsok.com/states-poet-laureate-dies/article/2606347. Accessed June 19, 2013.

Selected Poems by Betty Lou Shipley

Churchyard

To all strangers to the family plot:
Do not worry. These fires are all out
and who is left to measure the life
between two dates—all the little ones

unnamed and winterborn, the traveler's
baby, hangers-on through wars
and trouble, whose plows grew old
in the earth, and flowers long

since picked as young girls, too soon faded
and overblown. Here a line, there a thread
thrown across the gulf. Is this the earth
the poor inherit, cold common stone?

If I say them wrong, love is the excuse.
And for all their small detonations,
even here in this remembered earth
things hum and change.

And there is none unquiet, under this
singing a festival of bones, these
dead and buried, risen again
as old poems.

I Know Why Alton Speakman
Hanged Himself in the Marietta Jail

April 7, 1930
Love County News
"Young Marietta Man Hangs Self"

His sister said, "Alton
don't take on so.
It's only for three days.
The good Lord knows you got drunk
and broke the winder outen the feed store.
It ain't as if it's the crime of the century.
Every one celebrates some
when they come 21.
When you get home we'll fix you
some good ole chicken and dumplins
and forget all about this. Even mama
is gettin' over her mad.

Alton just said, "Ellie,
I cain't stand to be
shut up somewhere I cain't
get out of." and the next morning
they found him swinging
from the overhead pipes,
stepped off his bunk in the jail cell
with his belt tied
around his neck.

Alton, Alton, that we were 14
was no excuse, nor is "kids
will be kids." Why is there always
one who gets all the worst of us,
some devilish pecking order?

It was my idea to steal the beer
and take it to Harjo cemetery.

The others just went along,
even mine to dare you
to look into the gaping grave,
to open the door to the tool shed
where we swore the body was waiting,
just one peek would prove the unproveable
once
and for all,
my idea to push you into the dark
and drop the latch.
We turned on your screams and ran
laughing
ran thinking you would get quiet,
get mad any minute.

He screamed
it seems for seven years
and tumbled bloody at our feet
babbling,
nails broken and torn at the door,
knees raked raw on the splintered floor.
Helpless and puzzled in the corner stood
tall old Mr. Tinsley,
wakened from a stolen snooze
in the tool shed after opening a grave
for the city.
How was I to know?
But I know why Alton Speakman
hanged himself
in the Marietta jail.

Perfect Attendance

Kathy Ann Wilson's stone is pink
new and heart-shaped
standing out from other markers like a flower
in weeds
and she was a flower among children,
won a pin on Easter for perfect attendance
at Sunday school, and last week
at the Freewill Baptist Church summer revival
she never missed a night.
Brother Bob preached fire and love
and hell and miracles alternately
pounded his limp Bible and held it aloft
like an exhausted bird,
and when the congregation sang the invitation
Just as I am . . .
tearful sinners under heavy conviction
stumbled up the aisle to Jesus.
Brother Bob saved souls all over Lincoln County.
Kathy Ann came to Jesus the first night,
felt the Holy Spirit move through Brother Bob's
electric hand.
When he told of Jesus walking upon the waters
she could feel the cold sure lift of water
on the bottoms of her feet.
She was raised with others from the consecrated water
of Bell Cow Creek, a new creature in Christ.
Sins rolled away down the muddy river.
"Let's play Jesus,"
she said to a friend come over to play,
arranging an old blue bedspread around her shoulders,
"We'll walk on water. I'll be first."

She strolled serenely down the path
to the pond nodding to invisible followers
chatting with the disciples near the persimmon tree,
out to the end of the dock,
turned magnificently, arms raised
then stepped off
dropped
like a stone
into the deep
cold
waters
of faith.

Old Riddles

Why do their memories grow
thin as strings on a harpsichord, indistinct
and distant as someday. Why do they
take leave of earth so often
out of a sudden chill in advance of morning
leaving a revenge of possessions, years
of towels saved for good, boxes
of buttons one dares not discard
and in their cellars, jars of fruit
no one cares to eat or throw away,
trunk after trunk of quilts, doilies crocheted
and crocheted, buried with tatting and crewel
deep in sweet dry scent of the very old
with volumes of yellowed photographs
dim, unnamable riddles.

Why

spend another evening here with Jay Leno
or David Letterman. I'm going to check out
of this overpriced row house straight
into the nearest Holiday Inn. Then I'll run
myself out on the high board and belly flop
into the unreal green for the second time
in my life. That should wake me up. Then
I'll get into my smartass Honda and drive by
Kickingbird Theater where the brats congregate
and stare back at ninth graders I used to worry
through gerunds and infinitives, and I'll park
in front of the Interurban Café, pick up some
quesadillas to go then find my dark way out
to the lake, to the promontory near the dam
where we tossed the ashes of the prettiest girl
our family ever produced, and I am going
to remember the sudden way the wind
changed and blew her back into our eyes
into our hearts, as if
as if she didn't want to leave us
and I am going to remember that
when I left the lake I was wearing Jennifer
white and glorious on my favorite black sweater.

Because in the Context of Transition
Someone in my Poetry Class Asked
If I Really Would Like to Meet Jesus—
Now

Yes
I would leave you, right here
in the middle of metaphor swinging
between two balanced contentions, would
depart this world minus contrail
for upper rooms, be gone without so much
as a twinkle, no question of smoke
or mirrors, gone like a failed simile,
out of mind, without resolution or conclusion.

Sans last line, I would go, take leave
as from intensive care, machinery
wheezing and laboring behind me, gone
out of the busyness of inexact terms, done
with cities, over-peopled, scraping at the sky
my poem finished, out of here, over
and I do not wave good-bye. Now
somebody say Amen!

1998–2001

JOE RUSSEL KREGER

When Betty Shipley passed away in March 1998, Oklahoma was left without a poet laureate. Soon after her passing, Governor Frank Keating—at the urging of Dr. Charles Freeman, the state's Secretary of Agriculture—named cowboy poet Joe Kreger to the position, asking him to finish out Shipley's term and appointing him to serve his own two-year tenure. Unfortunately for some, Kreger's work looked backward to a more innocent time at the dawn of a new millennium. This, however, may have been the point: Kreger's faith-based values and cowboy heritage allowed Oklahomans to acknowledge their storied past before venturing into an uncertain future, one still marred by the violence of the 1995 Oklahoma City bombing and its aftermath.

Like his immediate predecessors Carol Hamilton and Betty Shipley, Kreger came to writing poetry late, "out of frustration," at age 56. As he remembers, "The Salt Fork of the Arkansas River where our ranch headquarters is located kept flooding and tearing us up. I got a poem in my head about it, wrote it down, and I guess I sprang a leak of my own because I've been at it ever since." Although he had not been officially writing poetry for very long, regional fame came when he called into AgriTalk, a nationally syndicated radio show broadcast from Iowa. The discussion topic that day concerned the meaning of happiness in rural life. Even though the program did not allow poems to be read on air, the producer, Rustin Hamilton, made an exception when Kreger recited his "Small Pleasures of Life" to him over the phone during a commercial break. Impressed with the poet's humility, Hamilton made an exception, Kreger read his poem on air, and the program received over 1,000 responses. Hamilton subsequently became Kreger's literary agent and has helped him develop into a phenomenon among Oklahoma's ranching and poetry communities, setting up more than 100 readings for him at farm meetings, churches, charity events, and hospitals. As one can guess, these developments came as a complete surprise to a rancher nearing his sixties. Much in Kreger's background, however, belies such a reaction; he should not have been so surprised.

Joe Russel Kreger was born on August 22, 1939, in Tonkawa, Oklahoma, the town in which he still resides. Although Hamilton describes his work as "simple poetry from a simple guy," that portrayal does a disservice to Kreger's parents and upbringing. His father, Glen Kreger, was a country doctor originally from Pennsylvania, and his mother, Gladys Kreger, was a homemaker originally from Kansas who had completed her freshman year of college. Because of his parents' backgrounds, Kreger was raised in an educated household with access to books and other intellectual amenities atypical of many ranching families. His father, especially, instilled in him a love of poetry and supported his son's academic work at Northern Oklahoma College (NOC) and Oklahoma State University, the latter of which he graduated from in 1961. Although he served briefly in the Army, Kreger has spent most of his life raising cattle in Arkansas, on his parents' farm, or on land leased from his neighbors. To supplement his income at times, he has sold ranch equipment, worked at Continental Oil Company, and taught agriculture courses at NOC. However, on horseback is where he feels most comfortable. "Ranchin'," living off the earth, is where he feels most at home.

This fact is apparent in his two poetry books, *Lookin' at Life* (1997) and *Still Lookin'* (2000), the latter a finalist for the Oklahoma Book Award for poetry in 2001. In both volumes, Kreger depicts the joys and woes of everyday rural life. Large by conventional poetry standards, *Lookin' at Life* collects fifty-nine narrative poems organized in ten different sections, the titles of which provide an overview of Kreger's unpretentious concerns: *Family, Workin', Observin', Eatin', Nature, Critters, Lookin' Back, Pardners, Getting' Older,* and *Lookin' Up.* While most of the topics and themes of the book are typical of the cowboy poetry genre, a special moment occurs when Kreger recounts the passing of his daughters Sara and Dessa in "The Girls on Loan from God." As expressed in the poem, Kreger dealt with their death from an automobile accident in 1985 by embracing his faith, acknowledging that they were "on loan" to him and his wife Pat until God called them back home to heaven. The next two poems deal with the girls individually: "Sara's Babies" recounts his oldest daughter's approach to hand-feeding calves, and "Dessa's Airplane Ride" expresses Kreger's regret at never paying for his youngest daughter to ride in the sky as promised. Lighter moments, however, do occur and make up a large portion of the book. "Our Neighbors to the South" exploits the Texas/Oklahoma rivalry by making fun of Texans' braggadocio; "That Gremlin in My Shed" blames a mischievous creature for missing objects around the Kreger ranch; and "Free Meals?" shows that food is the only good reason to attend an agricultural sales presentation. Although many of Kreger's poems are light in nature, others are intentionally didactic. As the poet states, "Personally, I enjoy drawing a lesson or principle of life out of situations. Most of my poems are on values and observations of life, and lessons learned from just observing horses, dogs and cows." For the most part, Kreger employed this same method of composition for his second back, *Still Lookin'*, which, in length and subject matter, acts as a companion to the first.

Due to Kreger's narrow thematic scope, much of *Still Lookin'* is redundant in content. Included is another sentimental poem about his daughters, "The Windbreak" (the poet's personal favorite), as well as more poems on ranching, God, and animals. Subsequently, his stubborn adherence to repetitive verse forms and regular rhyme schemes make his work more reminiscent of Delbert Davis and Rudolph Hill than of his sophisticated contemporaries. As suspected, there are few surprises here except for the lack of individual sections. Instead, Kreger organizes these poems alphabetically, which creates thematic ruptures in the book and an assumed nonchalance from the poet. A pleasant surprise, however, does occur in "Olde Bovine," which Kreger wrote in response to being named Oklahoma's 13th Poet Laureate. In the poem's epigraph, Kreger wittingly admits that he feels "a need to upgrade [his] writing style. Noting that many of the great classic poems were composed in Old English, [he] decided to try this format [. . .]" for a change. Even though Kreger is incorrect in stating that many of England's poets wrote in Old English, he attempts to compose a poem about a wondering cow in the style of

17th century England. While this attempt illustrates Kreger's humility over his appointment, it also aligns with the perception of the "poet laureate" title by the general public, most of whom equate it with the arrogance and pomposity of English royalty (as this book's introduction aptly illustrates). Because of this identification with his audience, Kreger's books have sold several thousands of copies. Such popularity has also allowed him to record three compact discs of material—*Small Pleasures*, *The Code*, and *Gatherin' Strays*—all of which are available from the *High Plains Journal* website.

The fact that Joe Kreger is able to maintain humor in the face of adversity says a lot about his tenacious personality and his faith in God. Not only did he lose his ranch due to financial difficulties, but his only living child, Joe Jr., now suffers from multiple sclerosis. Recently, the poet himself has been slowed by prostate cancer. Although he has faced many difficult times, Joe Kreger still remains positive. His poem "The Road Still Runs Both Ways" illustrates the code that he lives by, one where a man is judged by his treatment of others, earning a reputation for politeness and honesty that will eventually outlive him. For expressing such positive values in a cynical era, Kreger's work should be read and appreciated.

Oklahoma's cowboy culture would have remained absent from the poet laureate position without Joe Kreger's presence. As he states, his appointment to the position "affirmed that his work expresses the traditional values that Oklahoma's culture most embodies." For this reason, he wants to be remembered as an "Okie poet" rather than as a "cowboy poet." Doing him this honor will indeed show that his poetry is appreciated throughout Oklahoma.

Selected Bibliography

Primary Works
Kreger, Joe. *Lookin' at Life*. Kansas City: Innovative Broadcast Corporation, 1997.

———. *Still Lookin'*. St. Louis: Doane Agricultural Services Company, 2000.

Secondary Works

"2001 Oklahoma Book Award Finalists." Oklahoma Center for the Book. Accessed July 8, 2013. <http://www.odl.state.ok.us/ocb/01final.htm>. Accessed July 8, 2013.

Root, Ken. "Joe Kreger: My Most Unforgettable Character." *High Plains Journal*. Dec. 12, 2005. http://www.hpj.com/archives/2005/dec05/dec12/JoeKreger-Mymostunforgettab.cfm. Accessed July 8, 2013. Accessed July 8, 2013.

Shumpert, Doreen. "Joe Kreger—Cowboy Poet." *Eclectic Horseman*. April 10, 2008. <http://www.bonsallbuckingbulls.com/articles/20070629221250.html>. Accessed July 11, 2013.

Selected Poems Joe Russel Kreger

The Salt Fork

Joe Kreger's first poem, written in 1995.

I've been through drouths and oil field fires
and had calves die of the crud.
But, I never felt more helpless
than watchin' The Salt Fork flood.

In times long past, she built up this land
that borders her windin' path.
She nourished the crops and sheltered wild game,
never showin' her latent wrath.

Then, back in the day of the WPA,
they tamed her with the Salt Plains dam.
But, as years went by, and the lake silted up,
her submission proved only a sham.

Folks in the bottom kinda thought of her
as an old and trusted friend.
For forty years, a benevolent stream
that quietly flowed 'round the bend.

Neighbors would meet upon her banks,
engagin' in friendly chats.
They'd picnic on her sandy bars
And noodle her flathead cats.

The sixties brought progress like bridges and roads,
and they came through with I-35.
The new bridge choked the path she would use,
when she decided to come alive.

In '73, she woke up from her nap,
and her fury, she revealed.
She gathered up force like a tidal wave,
never sparing a bottomland field.

She washed out the new road and ravished the land,
spreadin' sand and debris as she chose.
Why she'd waited so long to show she was strong,
Only the Good Lord knows.

Ever since that time, every few years,
she flexes her muscle at will,
washin' out dikes, coverin' crops
and lettin' her wild waters spill.

She floods folks' homes with a fiendish glee
as she roars and swirls through their lands.
She couldn't give a hang 'bout my neighbors and me,
nor the work we've done with our hands.

I know that I can't control her,
'cause I'm only a mortal man.
So, I just try to keep a watchful eye
And respond in the best way I can.

When the black storms gather in the western sky,
and we know Grant County's catchin' rain,
we start gettin' ready 'cause we know what we do
can sure save a great heap of pain.

As the water starts backin' down the ditch to the west,
and the brome field goes out of sight,
I know it's time to start movin' cows,
And I pray that it's not at night.

I ride belly deep in water
pushin' cattle up to the rim.
My fingers choke the saddle horn,
'cause I never learned how to swim.

When the cattle are safe, we head for the barn
to salvage our supplies.

We get out what we can in this frustratin' race
with a river that's on the rise.

She'll gather strength from the rains upstream,
and breach the levy with her flood.
Then, she starts to cut and ream,
her torrent laced with mud.

That's when I start feelin' helpless,
'cause all I can do is watch
as she expands her domain and converts the terrain
into one big watery splotch.

I don't like to show emotion,
but I just have to let out a sigh,
as I witness her waters coverin' up
our winter hay supply.

Sometimes I feel like a subject
to this wild Riparian Queen,
who enforces her rule on this bottomland fool
with her waters fierce and mean.

If you could take a river to court,
she'd be branded a true outlaw,
the rebellious harlot daughter
of the mighty Arkansas.

The Girls on Loan from God

In a celestial meeting,
the Almighty gave a nod
and dispatched His host of angels
to bring the girls on loan from God.

They were sent into this world
from that land that's free from sin.
Dessa and Sara came here to us,
and George and Judy got Loralynn.

We were such proud parents,
and we loved them as our own,
but we had to learn an eternal truth—
they were only here on loan.

We nurtured them from infancy
to the first blush of womanhood.
There were many trials along the way,
but those days were, oh, so good.

The brief and fleeting time we had
to look upon each precious face
was only an expression
of God's enduring grace.

When the day arrived for their return
back to from whence they came,
our hearts were nearly broken,
and we yearned for our world to stay the same.

But the comforter came down to us
and brought us to submission.
He showed us that this was in the Plan,
and the girls had filled their mission.

My belief is that we parted
when their allotted time was spent,
and their departing situation
was not an accident.

God's truth is sometimes hard,
and I must now confess
that children are ours to love and train,
but not ours to possess.

And though they have departed
into the Great Hereafter,
this world is now a better place
for having heard their laughter.

And we rest in assurance
that, when our last earthly steps are trod,
we again will be united
with the girls on loan from God.

Our Neighbors to the South

They're often accused of tellin' tall tales
and runnin' off at the mouth,
but I have lots of friends amongst 'em,
our neighbors to the south.

They really like to tell Okie jokes,
so I retaliate with a misnomer.
I like to refer to their native state
as "Baja Oklahomer."

The Road Still Runs Both Ways

Son, just let me tell you
some important facts of life.
In dealin' with your fellow man,
they'll save a heap of strife.

When you're doin' any kind of business,
tradin' horses or sellin' cows,
think in terms of the Golden Rule,
not just what the law allows.

You need to make some money
while you are workin' your plan,
but leave the other guy a little—
don't make it all on one man.

The Bible says not to muzzle your ox
while he is treadin' out grain,
so when you have partners or are workin' hands,
pay 'em their fair share of your gain.

Protect your reputation
for now and years beyond.
Speak only the truth when you're dealin',
and make your word your bond.

Another thing I know
that will help you to get along—
stand up forever when you're right,
but back down when you're wrong.

This final thought I leave you
to stay with you all of your days,
no matter whether you're buyin' or sellin',
the road still runs both ways.

Olde Bovine

Upon being considered for appointment as Poet Laureate of Oklahoma, I began to feel a need to upgrade my writing style. Noting that many of the great classic poems were composed in Old English, I decided to try this format in my very next poem. The poem makes a good case for me to go back to writing in "Olde Okie."

Where didst thou goest, Olde Bovine?
Thou surely art the wandering kind.
I riseth early, stayeth late
because thou chose the wrong dang gate.

I seeketh thee to no avail
as I pursue thy winding trail.
Thou didst escapeth, now do flee,
thy sorry offspring follerin' thee.

To capture thee is now a must.
I trail thy footprints in the dust.
Thou leadeth me through thickest brush.
My noble steed goes in a rush.

My relationship with thee I ponder
as I see thy tracks go over yonder.
Mine agony wouldst be cut in half
if thou wouldst have a decent calf.

But, when I saw thee last in early fall,
thou led a scrawny, runt hairball.
And, though my brand is on thy hide,
thou dost not fill mine eyes with pride.

Thou consumeth my expensive feed.
Thou hooketh at my favorite steed.
Thou bloweth snot in my back pocket.
Thou cleareth gates just like a rocket.

Thy refuse splatters on my raiment.
Thou will not meet my bank note payment.
I board thee at an annual loss.
Thou won't recover thy first cost.

I'll find thee yet, O sorry snide.
Onward through the brush I ride.
I leaneth forward, spur my steed.
I shall close up thy two-day lead.

Insanely now, I start to laugh.
I'll rid thee of thy sorry calf.
And, when my loop ensnares thy rack,
I'll convert thy flesh to a lean Big Mac.

But, soon I sober, gaze around.
I've lost thy footprints on the ground.
The sinking sun sets on my sorrow.
I must resume my search tomorrow.

Once more, thou hast escaped my reach
and filled my mouth with profane speech.
I curse thee and thy bad offspring.
Will I get caught before the spring?

I seek the day, O Surly Beast,
when thou becomes a burger feast.
But, until that blessed day arriveth,
I'll chase the on, (if I surviveth).

2001–2003

CARL BRAUN SENNHENN

When Maryland native Carl Sennhenn was appointed to the poet laureate position in 2001, Governor Frank Keating could not have chosen an individual more opposite from his predecessor, Joe Kreger. While Kreger is a self-proclaimed "Okie" poet who writes rhymed cowboy poetry for rural farmers and ranchers, Sennhenn is a college professor who writes meta-poems in free verse on such existential questions as the meaning of life, the experience of time, and the different ways people face death. Fortunately, Sennhenn's commission began a trend of appointing sophisticated, worldly poets to the position, a succession that includes such well-known names as Francine Ringold, N. Scott Momaday, and Jim Barnes. This new attention to quality not only lent the Oklahoma poets laureate more credibility nationwide but also gave the position greater appreciation in the state at the start of the new millennium.

Carl Sennhenn was born in Baltimore, Maryland, on May 24, 1936, to George Carl Sennhenn, an American of Swiss heritage who worked at the United States Experimental Station in Annapolis during World War II, and Olga Henrietta Braun Sennhenn, a child of naturalized American citizens of German heritage. As a child in Annapolis, Sennhenn spent much of his time alone, which manifested itself later in the contemplative nature of his verse. For much of his childhood, he was bed-ridden with pneumonia or asthma, which caused him to miss grammar school for long periods of time, making it difficult to forge friendships with other children. While convalescing in bed, however, he read many books, generating an appreciation for writers and their craft. When not ill, Sennhenn often visited nearby Severn River and the Truxton Woods, contemplating the natural world in further solitude. These short bicycle trips helped him appreciate different varieties of flora and fauna, which appear today in his deeply meditative poems.

This cling to solitude changed, however, in 1951, when George Sennhenn moved the family to Oklahoma City when he began a new job at Tinker Air Force Base. Here, Carl enrolled in John Marshall High School. At first, he was "confused by the immediate friendliness of classmates," but the teenager soon came out of his shell and made friends with his peers, many of whom he keeps in touch with today. It was here, during his junior year, that he began to write creatively, composing a book of poems for teacher Mary Lois Boorom.

After high school, Sennhenn moved to Norman, where he has lived ever since, enrolling at the University of Oklahoma for his undergraduate and graduate work. In late 1960, he began to compose poetry seriously towards the end of working on his master's degree in English. As he relates,

> not until I had nearly completed graduate studies did I begin writing poetry with any degree of seriousness or frequency. On reflection, I think any serious attention to my own writing came at periods of transition in my life: the end of high school, the end of graduate study, the beginning of my professional life. So I find in my poems that I often deal with transition: from grief to joy, from joy to grief, from ignorance to understanding, etc., and I hope the images and metaphors that fill my work suggest to readers the university of my personal experiences in such a way as to encourage them to write, not necessarily poetry, and to embrace experience with an understanding and appreciation for life's infinite variety.

Especially influential on his early poetry was John Donne, the subject of his master's thesis. Titled "Within the Meditative Tradition: A Study of John Donne's *Devotions Upon Emergent Occasions*," Sennhenn's thesis examines one of Donne's few prose pieces, which, he argues, should be considered not only "as a meditative experience or as theology" but also as literature. The influence of Donne and the metaphysical poets can be found in Sennhenn's lyric poems today, especially in his use of extended metaphors, meditations, and wittiness. No doubt, Sennhenn was attracted to *Devotions Upon Emergent Occasions* by empathizing with Donne's concept of refreshing the soul through sickness and suffering.

Having grown fond of the academic way of life, Sennhenn became a faculty member at Rose State College in Midwest City, teaching courses in English and the humanities for more than fifty years. Although he had been writing poetry seriously since 1960, his first chapbook, *Harvest of Life*, did not appear until 1987 when he was 51 years old. This lag in publication was due to Sennhenn's teaching duties and his love of traveling. Two years later, his second chapbook, *The Center of Noon* (1989) was published. Both of these volumes established the themes that Sennhenn would explore in more depth later: the ways in which personal memory creates nostalgia, the absences in life left by death, the difficulties and joys of teaching, and the intimate process of writing referentially. In his most recent books, *Travels Through Enchanted Woods* (2006) and *Nocturnes and Sometimes, Even I* (2012) these topics come to full bloom, showing that the poet is still growing in sophistication and introspection as he approaches age 80.

In *Travels Through Enchanted Woods*, the winner of the 2007 Oklahoma Book Award for poetry, Sennhenn uses epigraphs to acknowledge the influence of such other writers as John Donne, Anne Sexton, Raymond Carver, and Li-Young Lee. In these poems, he puts his unique spin on the genres, themes, and techniques established by these predecessors and contemporaries: "Oceans" and "Sea and Sky Terror" are meditative poems in the vein of Donne; "Pacific: First Views" and "Really Swift and Fine" express Sexton's brand of confessionalism; "Campfire Reverie," written in memory of Carver, presents the causes of and excuses made for alcoholism; and "The Life the Poet Creates is His Poem" and "Leaving the Egyptian Tapestry" exhibits Lee's interest in fusing ancestry with deep images. Although his book could have ended up derivative, Sennhenn was able to put his own stamp on his poems, mostly through depictions of his experiences as a child, teenager, and adult. No doubt, the woods he mentions in his title are the Truxton Woods he visited as a boy, a forest that still fills his memories with enchantment.

While *Travels through Enchanted Woods* established Sennhenn as an important voice in Oklahoma, the publication of his most recent book, *Nocturnes and Sometimes, Even I*, should make him prominent on the national stage. In this volume, which won the 2013 Oklahoma Book Award for poetry, Sennhenn tackles such subjects as the relevance of personal history, the construction of "fictional" characters, the mimetic quality of signatures, and the perception of space in meta-poems that acknowledge their own origin, making universal questions relevant through personal reflection. Most significant, however, is his development of a new style, one that largely ignores punctuation. Although he does not compose using Charles Olsen's "field theory" of poetry, he has learned, extraordinarily, to compose by breath, making each line of his poems its own self-contained unit that works without the use of commas or periods. While many contemporary poets have attempted this technique—former Kentucky poet laureate James Baker Hall immediately comes to mind—Sennhenn is one of the few who employs it successfully. As *Nocturnes and Sometimes, Even I* shows, Sennhenn is still wildly inventive, changing his style dramatically the older he grows. The poet's success with this technique is even more amazing when one learns that he wrote the book in just over a year.

Although Carl Sennhen formally retired form Rose State College in 2008, he still remains busy by giving public readings and by teaching poetry through his former employer's Community Learning Center. As for his appointment as Oklahoma's fourteenth poet laureate, he writes that

> to be named Poet Laureate of Oklahoma in 2001 was completely a surprise, enabling me to find a wider audience than I had known before. I had taught creative writing classes for children at the Norman Firehouse Art Center and for senior adults at Rose State. Now I was invited to conduct workshops and do readings at various high schools [. . .] In addition, for more than ten years now, I have coordinated and hosted monthly poetry readings at the Studio for the Performing Arts in Norman. Although I cannot say I have initiated any programs, I have done my best to promote the cause of poetry and [to] encourage the efforts of others.

No doubt, Sennhenn's elderly years have been kind to him. As he says, people his age are "supposed to be called 'senior adults' [. . .] I'm the same age as them, but I don't worry about what I am. When you get to be 77, it doesn't make a lot of difference." Such a positive attitude on life and aging is surely part of the reason for his late critical success.

Selected Bibliography

Primary Works

Sennhenn, Carl. *The Center of Noon.* Norman: Poetry Around, 1989.

————. *Harvest of Light.* Norman: Poetry Around, 1987.

————. *Nocturnes and Sometimes, Even I.* Cheyenne, OK: Village Press Books, 2012.

————. *Oklahoma Voices: Carl Sennhenn.* Metropolitan Library System, 2007. CD.

————. *Travels Through Enchanted Woods.* Cheyenne, OK: Village Press Books, 2006.

Sennhenn, Carl Braun. "Within the Meditative Tradition: A Study of John Donne's *Devotions Upon Emergent Occasions.*" Diss. University of Oklahoma, 1960.

Secondary Works

"2013 Oklahoma Book Award Winner Carl Sennhenn to Read." Performing Arts Studios. http://www.pasnorman.org/programs/poetry/430-2013-oklahoma-book-award-winner-carl-sennhenn-to-read. Accessed July 22, 2013.

"Rose State College's Award-Winning Poet Experiencing 'Surge' of Creativity." *PRWeb.* June 1, 2013. http://www.prweb.com/releases/2013/6/prweb10786541.htm. Accessed July 22, 2013.

Two Master Poets, Carole Hamilton, Oklahoma Poet Laureate, 1995–1997 [and] Carl Sennhenn, Oklahoma Poet Laureate, 2001–2003: A Centennial Tribute. Dir. Maggie Abel and Charles Maupin. Magster TV, 2007. DVD.

Selected Poems by Carl Sennhenn

Mary and Sarah

The Daughters of God Quilting Circle
sews busily as Mary and Sarah
find a quiet spot to themselves. They talk.

Sarah speaks first.
"I watched them leave
that morning so long ago, Isaac's
hand in Abraham's. My child
turned his face to his father
with such trust that I cannot forget it."

"Abraham's spine was rigid as if iron
had replaced bone and muscle. I wanted
to cry out, 'Abraham, don't' and tear
Isaac from his father and run with him
into the hills. But I kept silence
when I could not name my fear."

To ease Sarah's heart, Mary reminds her:
"Isaac was spared. It was enough
that Abraham would have sacrificed your son.
God was satisfied."

"Some demands God has no right
to make of us," Sarah insists.
"Isn't it like a jealous god
to demand proof of absolute obedience
and just like a man to show it?
Surely God could have known by looking
into Abraham's heart. No, I cannot
forgive what Abraham could have brought
himself to do." Bold now
Sarah whispers, "I cannot forgive God. He
behaved badly."

Mary has known a mother's sorrow.
The Queen of Heaven long ago saw
her child, lowly born, miracle in a manger
ascend to His Father's throne, to sit
at His right hand, to judge the quick and the dead.

Evening clouds soften the light
breezes cool the shadows, fan the quilting noises away.
Mary remembers the brutal
crucifixion of her beloved son.
She had known it was to come.
She had known her role in the Mystery,
had known it long and pondered it always
in her heart. And even now, as her Son
reigns in His promised glory and all
that angelic choirs foretold has come to pass,
it grieves her as nothing else ever could.

There is nothing more to say
and so Mary and Sarah quilt
in the painful silence that is a mother's.

Ubi Sunt Puellae

As casually as they draw cashmere
Across their shoulders
Girls who wore lab books
Under their arms
Came to Botany class.
Lectures out of doors made plausible—
So did the hints of early frost—
An autumnal finery as variegated
As the stately leaves just turning on the Oval.
Meanwhile, bittersweetly, chrysanthemums in their beds
Played counterpoint
To the last warm scents of summer.

I envied them the elegance of their ease.
Apparently none of them regretted that they felt for leaf science
No passion that approached their pursuit of fashion.
They bore their *C*'s as weightlessly
As the lacquer on their nails
While my *B* I sweated
As awkwardly as a child the suit that
Circumstance makes imperative.

Where are those girls
Who dropped their books
As easily as they let cashmere fall from their shoulders?
These years their beauty,
and their ease, may be faded somewhat
(A brief season in transit,
Sic gloria mundi !)
But autumnally they return their daughters to alma maters
Whose ovals bear the repetition
The passing years make traditional.

Really Swift and Fine

Swift and fine
they may be, but
aerodynamic splendors can never
replicate what I remember:
rides home in the winter
dark. Cars then were lined overhead
with fabric that browned
and assumed the sweet
musk of tobacco and summer dust.
I like to recall too
the hard finish of tweed seatcovers.
But most of all
I long for that soft
light from the dashboard
on starless winter nights;
adult voices from the front seat—
talking softly
of the distance home.
Nothing else quite defines
what it meant once to speed safely
and cut through the dark.

Somehow I've lost the memory
of ends of rides
but retain sensations of
movement—
an ascension of sorts—
out of the car and then floating
up the stairs, words whispered, a kiss
and later awakening (the journey forgotten)
cozy and warm and
    miraculously
the sun in its accustomed place
on my bed.

Tree Top Vision

I sit seriously to read the past
   and to take
Notes for the future
   only to discover
My second-story perch among shelves of books
   near the windows
Allows me an expanse of view.
It is an early-autumn afternoon,
   still summer warm,
When I catch the very first red leaves of the season
   crowning a maple.
Sap has already begun its yearly plunge
   toward earth.
I am reminded that my mission's,
   like the tree in autumn,
To map the life-sustaining from books
   on libraries' second floors
To classrooms where it may nourish
   those without tree top vision.

Message

Surely
There is a message within
This message:
"Tom is in Newcastle
"Indiana
"With his grandmother. He will miss tonight
"And next Tuesday's class."
Tom's in Newcastle, and all's right with the world?
Thanksgiving, and home for the holiday?

Not just "out of town and will miss class"
But solidity of specification
      rich in suggestion:
   Grandma's cooking
      a turkey basted brown and gold, succulent, holiday-aromatic,
         perhaps a goose,
      regal in the center of steaming porcelain islands, of
         family silver, family resemblances, family jokes, and of
         good will inherited just as surely as the family name.

    Is Newcastle farmland beyond the paned windows, stretching
through miles of fields and trees and old dogs napping late in the
November sun, country roads (all leading home) crossing America's
heart?

Tom's in Newcastle
With grandmother and will miss tonight,
Tuesday too, arousing
No professional suspicion.
Still I ponder
The message
(for the heart)
Within.

Poetry While a Plumber Plumbs

This morning I've summoned
a plumber out among deep drifts
and ice-treacherous roads
to attend frozen pipes. While he
plies his trade, the most recent poems
of a laurelled and white haired master
have arrived and awakened me
to my craft. Out of paper
I write small in the margins of one
of his poems, and then out of margins
desperate I crowd smaller still
between his lines

Thus
this January morning
a strange sort of poetry
emerges between our words
My craft has met his art
just as the plumber
works his trade in white
and wintry spaces

Polyphemus

The office is dark
this afternoon
the two window walls
my only source of light

Reluctantly they admit
the afternoon
gray and dull shortly
before spring rain

I cultivate the sensation
of a cave, think of Polyphemus
imagine myself a kindly
Cyclops

No Odysseus
seeking gifts
arrives yet
vainglorious, bombastic

indifferent to any
need for solitude.

CARL BRAUN SENNHENN

The Ant and I

Too soon the hour has grown late
and I am wearied from long days toiling
through fields of minutiae: stacks of essays
that proliferated like weeds in summer
but, ignoring them, I am resolved
to complete one last task—revise
recent poems—before the drive home
Cursing the slow ineptness of fingers, I
surprise a brown ant, a Lilliputian creature
scurrying around and around the rim of my
    keyboard
before it changes direction, crawls over the keys
themselves to trace the outlines of their letters
Sometimes it even dives into the grooves between
    keys

Like ungraded essays, poems seem irrelevant

Intrigued, I cease all typo-prone activity to watch
and allow the ant to quest unimpeded, no Gulliver-
    clumsy
efforts to bother it. If it notices me watching, my
    eyes magnified
by glasses, perhaps I seem only a gentle kind of
    giant
who will permit it to complete in peace
a survey of this strange new geography
before it disappears as silently as it appeared

Poems will wait another day

The Observed

for Wayne Buchman

When we meet these days
an old college friend never
fails to bring something philosophical
to share. In our graduate school
world we swapped smokes
when the other was out
and sometimes complaints
about classes. Now he brings
from his retirement gems
from Eastern philosophy mined
in long afternoon and evening
reading. Just last week he
brought this—whose thought I
cannot recall—In our observation
of anything we can be changed
Then I remembered learning
years ago the act of observation
changes whatever we observe
Does observation, then, make possible
an exchange of energy so powerful
as to modify the molecular structure
of both observer and the observed
Is the energy of the observed
sufficient to affect being and behavior
Of the observer, perhaps even
his faith

Unsure of the answer, I am reminded of van Gogh's
Starry Night. It is possible that spinning
stars and moon in a vibrating heaven
are not matters of Vincent's style after all
but faithful representation of an observed night
of stars changed at least for the time it took
to paint them

Then, too, recent changes I have observed
in myself just possibly might be evidence
of an all-powerful observer, and my perception
of being observed, a sign
of grace

Curves

Sometimes . . . it's the curve of a chair that hurts you . . . . .

--Anne Sexton

Cushioned, the curve of a chair will not hurt.
Stark lines strike with purity
and blind to lesser joys.
Smoothness of finish and silence of wood
ask for touch
and so
you do and then, perhaps,
you hurt.

Other curves hurt, too;
the curve of horizon so transparent
from shores of the Pacific
that you ponder
earth, sky, and water—all the while
accepting the impossible other side.

Then there are curves
of flesh
of moon
of music
of leaf
all so simple
they can make you weep.

Sometimes, Even I

sometimes, even I
tip toe into poems
when too self-conscious
to call attention to Self
I come to see what
I have to say and when
too shy to step forward
I have become *he*, sometimes even
she if unwilling to sing
of love in my true voice. Then
when conflicted, I have retreated
to hide behind *they*

sometimes poems will reveal
a self as if standing door-framed
to be measured: how much
—or, perhaps, if—one has grown
at all since last season's
prose-benighted lines

yes, sometimes I may
steal into a poem
see what I have shared
then slip quietly behind
you, hoping to hear
your sigh-approving
Yes

2003–2007

FRANCINE LEFFLER RINGOLD (JOHNSON)

When Francine Leffler was born on February 16, 1934, she was thrust into an uncertain world, one where the instability of her parents' lives—her mother was a would-be dancer who died young—resulted in her being raised in Brooklyn and Manhattan by her aunt Isabel "Bea" Lubow and her husband, John Stevenson. While the loss of her mother at age 8 remains a major theme in her work, Francine was better off socially and economically by being raised by the Stevensons, who could provide her with a privileged upbringing. As a young woman, her aunt had toured the U.S., London, and Paris as a dancer, becoming known in the latter city as "the blond Josephine Baker." Having later studied fashion and costume design at New York University, she became involved with many Broadway productions and was eventually named to the board of the American Theatre Wing in 1957. Isabel's husband, John, was similarly influential in New York, having served as director and president of Greystone Publishing, one of the first direct mail publishers in the U.S. No doubt her aunt's and uncle's professions made a profound impact on Francine since she eventually became a professor of theater, literature, and creative writing at the University of Tulsa, where she taught for more than forty years.

Due to the challenging nature of her childhood, Francine wrote her first story at age 12 as a gift to her Uncle John, accompanying it with a pair of hand-knitted argyle socks. While the story concerned her uncle raising a daughter that was not biologically his, it was the process of making the socks that fascinated Francine and convinced her to continue writing. As she relates: "it was something about the complexity of the socks, the weaving, the pattern, that made me realize that a writer could do the same thing weaving different elements into a story. After that, it became a big fascination for me, not just telling the idea of a sequential narrative, but weaving all of these different elements into the same package." Although she had dabbled in dance like her mother and aunt, it was writing and teaching that would eventually become her lifelong vocations.

After graduating from Brooklyn's Midwood High School, Francine majored in English at the University of Michigan, where she met law student Anthony Ringold, a native of Tulsa. They wed in the Stevenson's home on June 7th 1955. Upon graduating that year, Anthony received a commission as an Army lieutenant. The couple subsequently lived in Fort Benning, Georgia, until he was de-commissioned. Afterward, Tony ended up relocating back to Tulsa, bringing his family with him. Francine has lived there ever since.

In the early 1960s, Francine Ringold took graduate courses at the University of Tulsa, where she also starting working for the *Nimrod International Journal of Prose and Poetry* as a reader of short story submissions under the tutelage of editor Winston Weathers. Although her master's thesis—entitled "The New Promethean"—analyzed Albert Camus' play *Caligula*, it was verse that became her chief creative interest. Subsequently, she published her first poem in 1964 at age 31, the same year she earned her master's degree.

After Weathers retired, Ringold became the editor-in-chief of *Nimrod* in 1966, growing it into one of the most acclaimed literary journals in the world. During her four decade tenure as editor, she published such important figures as Pablo Neruda, Octavio Paz, Stanley Kunitz, William Stafford, Rita Dove, and Mark Doty. She also brought attention to much world literature by publishing special issues that focused on such places as Central America, China, Vietnam, and the Soviet Union, giving many foreign authors their first publication in the United States.

Although *Nimrod* and her family of four children took up much of Ringold's time, she eventually earned her Ph.D. from the University of Tulsa in 1975. Once again, she returned to the subject of drama for her doctoral dissertation. Titled "Trial by Drama: From Fact to Rituals," this scholarly work—no doubt influenced by her aunt's background on Broadway and her own husband's work as a lawyer—

explores the ceremonial acts that connect drama with legal trials by focusing on plays that incorporate trial scenes as climactic events. Ringold writes that "[e]veryone seems to agree that trials are 'dramatic,' that the soul of the drama is the debate, the agon, the adversary system [. . .] The marriage of trial and drama is essential and not just circumstantial: Trial and drama both evolve from primitive ritual; they share a kinship with play; yet they are verbal arts, and serious systems for persuasion and for the demonstration and resolution of conflict. The potential power of two parallel structures prompts dramatists to continually renew their union."

While most dissertations languish in obscurity on library shelves, this volume's history shows that it has been read several times over the years, both at TU and at the UCLA School of Law. While Ringold would focus more on creative writing and teaching for the remainder of her life, this work shows her gift for literary criticism as well.

With her formal education finished at age 41, Ringold began the most creative period of her life, publishing books of poetry and a play, as well as books on creative writing, by local presses in Tulsa over the next thirty years. For the most part, her poetry is confessional, focusing on such topics as the importance of family and friends, lost memories, failing bodies, the problems of aging, and the ritualistic nature of dance. Ringold, however, is also politically aware, having written on such contemporary events as the second Gulf War, the Clarence Thomas confirmation hearings, and the bombing of the A. P. Murrah Building in Oklahoma City. A good example that fuses both concerns is the anti-war poem "Weaving Down the Court." Here, Ringold explores the intricate connection between sports and war by presenting America's feeling of "March madness" during the country's invasion of Iraq in 2003. The home audience yearns for victory in Iraq and on the basketball court as each set of players "fulfill" their "mission." The narrator's interest in these events stems from watching them unfold on television while waiting for a family member to give birth, wondering if the events will end in "death or birth" since both were "invented in bushes," alluding to women's vaginas, which birthed the participating players, and to 43rd President George W. Bush, who invented the rationale for the Iraq invasion. Such fusing of family occurrences with contemporary events is a hallmark characteristic of Ringold's work. Similarly, the poem "Wedding Song" connects family members to important historical figures by tracing the etymology of the names "David" and

"Elizabeth" throughout world history. As the couple prepares to marry, the narrator reminds them "[o]f this heritage, regal and earthbound, / [. . .] / a web stretched between past and present" that forever ties them to those who have come before.

Of Ringold's poetry books, the most notable are *The Trouble with Voices* (1995) and *Still Dancing: New and Selected Poems* (2005), both of which received the Oklahoma Book Award in 1996 and 2005, respectively. Also important is *Every Other One* (1999), a collaborative project she undertook with her second husband, Manly Johnson. Here, the couple depicts their life together in verse. Although they did not employ a formal process for composition, they often played off of each other's themes and images with "the last line of one poem" acting as "the impetus" for the following one, creating a unique reading experience for their audience.

Although the quality of her work alone warranted Ringold's appointment as Oklahoma's 15th poet laureate by Governor Brad Henry in 2003, her editorship of *Nimrod* and her commitment to community service also played important roles in the decision. Besides having taught in both the Oklahoma State Arts in Education and the Artists in the Schools programs, Ringold has also been devoted to supporting people with special needs throughout her career, which includes teaching at the Oklahoma School of the Deaf, the Tulsa Center for the Physically Limited, the Gatesway Foundation in Broken Arrow, and different senior citizen organizations. Out of these experiences came her two books on creative writing, *Making Your Own Mark: A Guide to Writing and Drawing for Senior Citizens* (1990), which she co-wrote with Madeline M. Rught, and *Writing and Painting at Gatesway* (1992). Such dedication to Oklahoma and its people no doubt resulted in Ringold being named to a second two-year term, the only poet laureate to receive the honor. While she continued with her community service activities in the post, she admits that

> nobody knows what the true role of the state poet laureate is. As she relates to interviewer Joe Myers: "[a]nd that is true with all the other state Poet Laureates that I have encountered. There aren't any rules. Your position is to promote poetry, but how you do it is up to you [. . .] So I went all around the state for poetry readings and the like."

This statement, of course, is too modest for Ringold who spent much of her time helping others in her adopted home state. Her awards and honors include serving as Humanities Scholar in Residence for KWGS-FM radio, working as an advisor to the Arts and Humanities Council in Tulsa, being named Newsmaker of the Year by Tulsa's Women in Communication, and being inducted into the Oklahoma Higher Education Hall of Fame. Along with Jennie Harris Oliver and Maggie Culver Fry, Ringold has been one of the most active poets laureate in the state's history. Unlike them, however, she is the first poet to hold a Ph.D. Because of her dedication to Oklahoma and its people, the state is better off for having Ringold as one of its citizens.

Although Francine Ringold often uses the term "feisty" to describe herself, she began slowing down as she approached age eighty. She was deeply affected by the death of her second husband and "soul-mate" Manly Johnson in November 2010. Three years later, she retired as editor of *Nimrod* after forty-seven years at the journal's helm. Today, she continues to write and teach when time allows. She also continues to serve *Nimrod* in an advisory capacity. Today, fans can find her on Facebook at least once a week, which she uses to keep in touch with family and friends.

Selected Bibliography

Primary Works

Ringold, Francine. *C. H. Rosenstein: 70 Years in the "Thickets of the Law."* Tulsa: Franson, 1985.

———. *The Healing Arts.* Tulsa: U of Tulsa, 2006.

———. *A Magic Journey: Writing and Painting at Gatesway.* Tulsa: Coman and Associates, 1992.

———. *Mercy: Mercy Otis Warren 1728–1814*, a one-act play. Tulsa: Johnson, 1987.

———. *The Muse of Attachment.* Tulsa: U of Tulsa, 2005.

———. "'My Dear Friend,' Isaac Bashevis Singer: An Interview." *Studies in American Jewish Literature* 1 (1981): 160–68.

———. "Roundabout Joyce." *James Joyce Quarterly* 12, no.4 (1975): 457–59.

———. *Voices.* Tulsa: Hadassah, 1981.

Ringold, Francine, and Madeline M. Rught. *Making Your Mark: A Drawing and Writing Guide for Senior Citizens.* Tulsa: Out on a Limb, 1990.

Ringold, Francine Leffler. *Still Dancing: New and Selected Poems.* Tulsa: Coman and Associates, 2005.

Ringold-Johnson, Francine, and Manly Johnson. *Every Other One.* Tulsa: Coman and Associates, 1999.

Ringold-Johnson, Francine Leffler. *The Trouble with Voices.* Tulsa: Council Oak, 1995.

Secondary Works

"Dr. Francine Ringold: Oklahoma Poet Laureate." The Oklahoma Center for Poets and Writers. Accessed Oct. 25, 2013. <http://poetsandwriters.okstate.edu/OKauthor/ringold.html>.

"Francine Leffler Becomes Engaged." *New York Times*. New York Times, May 15, 1955. Web. Oct. 25, 2013.

"Francine Leffler Wed." *New York Times*. New York Times, June 8, 1955. Web. Oct. 25, 2013.

"The University of Tulsa's Francine Ringold Named Poet Laureate of Oklahoma." The University of Tulsa. July 2, 2003. <http://www.utulsa.edu/academics/colleges/henry-kendall-college-of-arts-and-sciences/Departments-and-Schools/Department-of-English/News-Events-and-Publications/News/2003/July/TheUniversityofTulsasFrancineRingoldNamedPoetLaureate of Oklahoma.aspx>. Accessed: Oct. 25, 2013.

Selected Poems by Francine Ringold

The Trouble with Voices
for Anita Hill

St. Joan had trouble with voices.
   From the time she was ten,
'till the day they watched her burn
   the voices persisted.
They would kick her name
   into her right ear:

                            "...Joan
You are the chosen ..."   "...Joan
   will crown a King."   "...Joan
will mount a steed ... romp
   proudly at Orleans."

And then there was
   ... Claire of Assisi ...
She's still there for us to see,
   entombed in glass, her ash face
hands and ravaged teeth proclaiming:

Here is one who heard voices ...
   promising voices ... words
that pulled flowers from her womb;
   the flowers turned to sticks,
frogs leapt from the deepest caves
   of her being, strings encased in lead
twined from her belly. The voices railed:

"Name us as you are named!"
   And as she felt the hard knot swell,
she signed "welcome" to the order of the chosen,
   to those who hear their name called,
who believe they will not burn, and burn
   more surely ... more brilliantly,
      than all the rest.

Wedding Song

for Elizabeth and David

Of David we have splendid reference:
the small one who made Goliath pale,
the Saint of Wales,
the King of Scotland—even
David, the painter, both Gerard and Jacques—
David of Brown, David of Susan.

And Elizabeth, First—or if not first, most
famous—Elizabeth the Queen, Shakespeare's muse,
Raleigh's concubine (what? in that unwashed gown?).
And Elizabeth of the New Testament, mother of John;
and poet, Elizabeth of Romania, also Queen
like that one of Ireland and Britain, wife of George;
Elizabeth II, daughter of same, and Elizabeth
Petrovna of Russia, surely kin of Goodman, and if kin
then kind, and kin too of Sadie, she of Lvov,
schooled, as legend has it, by an Uncle, tutor to the Czar,
she too of Vineland, near Elizabethtown,
Great grandmother of us all, who blessed
Big John in his black sweater and Isabelle
still in her dancing shoes,
their concord to be complex and hearty.

Of this heritage, regal and earthbound,
a threadlike afterimage remains,
a web stretched between past and present,
each new strand quivering with light.
Look now! It shines still brighter.

Job's Wife

I've been thinking of Job's wife.
Her name must have been Sarah or Niobe
—though they don't tell us—
How she must have said, as she brushed
the tangles from her daughter's
long black hair: "Vanity must suffer!"
And so it does. I've been thinking
then of Sarah, for twenty years
married to Job, Sarah —
indignant because she knew
He (note the capital H please) had no right
to test the family that way, the children
abused and starved and murdered,
the plagues and sores and sickness,
the demolition, the mushroom cloud of agonies —
Sarah vented her fury. And he, Job,
how he had taken it, had assumed his guilt,
had bowed his head in humility and abjection,
said: "Thy will be done!"
asked: "What have I done, O Lord?"
When Sarah knew he had just lived well.

Was that his crime then? To live well?
Was it necessary to shove a message in his face,
to make women and children and animals of the field
suffer in order to see, to acknowledge
the incomprehensible workings of the universe?
Sarah had no patience with abstraction:
she insisted, prodded, even screeched:
"Touch this burning flesh!
"Feel the flailed skin as it falls back,
"Taste the brittle bones as they crumble,
bleached by the sun.
Then, Curse God and die!" she said.
Yet they both lived.

The Flume Maker

He saw the way the Romans did it:
stones placed upright in the ground
so time would have trouble
wearing the road down.
He only had bricks that would turn to dust,
but he placed them as carefully
as a mother touching a tip of cotton
to her nursing infant's lips,
promising, "Just this,
I will do this, just this,
then stop."

He placed each manicured brick,
first in the earth to measure the plot,
then lovingly lifting each red marker
packing in the cement,
laying rectangular stones, head to toe,
tongue and groove, dovetailing the corners,
pressing down a stubborn joint to make a perfect fit.
The days were hot and humid.
He worked out there, scored by the sun.
From her cool house, under glass,
she watched. The flume
widened like a waiting womb.
When rain came, it closed over his hand.
He would not stop.

When he finished, and the flume
ready to receive the sea
of rain and salt and snow,
she went, finally, out into the heat,
carefully pried up each brick,
to keep him at work,
to keep him alive,
out there in the sun.

O Mighty City

for the survivors of the April 19, 1995 bombing of the A. P. Murrah Building in Oklahoma City and all who build and rebuild, city upon city.

Between these branches
Egyptians built a city
dry as the sun, on the horizon
where we meet.
We are standing on a roof
bombed out by time.
The debris of humanity,
garbage and night soil,
fertilizes other fields;
the shards remain.
We throw them in a heap.
They multiply.
We are never rid of them:
these granite coffins
for animals, these tombs
of old kingdoms that rise
from the heart of the delta.

How, they asked themselves,
can a foundation last?
If we build a box, will it keep
the sand from shifting?

I am speaking here of time
and other phenomena;
I am speaking of a good
harvest of corn and flax.
I am speaking, mostly,
of stone of Luxor,
Of this City, of a fierce animal
screaming in the night.
I am speaking of the desert
into which the Nile has cut its way;
of recent excavations; of the remains

of ivory tusks, of she-goddesses
crowned with cow horns and the moon,
of ancient limbs dancing in bas-relief;
of bronze helmets and swords
imbedded with sapphires.
I am speaking of how
there is more under the ground
than above and how
we are still searching.

Weaving Down the Court

March 2003: New York, Spokane, Iraq
The night of the U.S. invasion of Iraq

A night to remember,
not cliché but numinous,
wild and unpredictable . . .
neither quite game nor "reality":
New York, LizLiz in hospital,
David by her side, cell phone carrying
voices over Spokane as Danté
flies down court to fulfill his mission.
On split screen, Iraq, tanks
streaming like tears on a sandy horizon.

A three-pointer, a two;
pains getting closer together as
March madness invades the Garden,
while in the desert, men
drop from the sky, not
gently from the silk
folds of the wombs of women,
but torn by helicopter blades,
shouting, "God is on our side,
God is on our side."

No surprise then that romance
begged from background music,
becomes so charming it is discordant,
slides into a spirit band salute,
a tin drum cavalcade
beating out the rhythm of nine months of labor:
Amani, Ella, Ibrahim, Yusef, Davis, Parker . . .
A convergence of cries, born of miracle of precision,
luminous like a clock, numbers mounting in crazed dedication
to causes invented in bushes, or dark caverns of ego,
yet each cry a call, each call a reminder:
This is not a staging.
This is the real thing.
This will be death or birth.

Delivery
  for Tony

Remember when Leslie was born,
plucked from my womb squalling?
You wanted to watch the delivery
but were ushered out. I waited
that night and into the morning
for your call. And John, how
he was placed, fists pounding,
on my breast? Remember? You
watched the players ram heads into other
stomachs. And Jim, delivered at night?
I could not see the wonder
of his shape emerging until now
with Suzanne, her black hair,
pressed wet and shining,
into my arms.

We are often alone, it seems,
at the best moments, moments
when miracles spring into our laps.
Perhaps that is the way it should be:
the gift of a moment, after years or months
of waiting, arises full blown,
like Venus from the waves:
Each daughter, each son,
Living.

2007–2009

N. SCOTT MOMADAY

In 2007, Oklahoma celebrated its centenary of statehood. To commemorate the occasion, Governor Brad Henry appointed N. Scott Momaday as the 16th poet laureate, bestowing on him the official title of Oklahoma Centennial State Poet Laureate. Although born in Lawton in 1934, Momaday had live out of state for decades but had just relocated back to Oklahoma so that his wife, Barbara, could receive cancer treatment at the OU Medical Center in Norman. The fact that he was the best known poet born in the state surely played a major role in the Henry's decision since he had won the 1968 Pulitzer Prize for fiction with his novel *House Made of Dawn* and had celebrated Oklahoma's southwestern landscape in *The Way to Rainy Mountain* (1976). Momaday's appointment was also fitting since he is of Kiowa, Cherokee, and English stock, all of which reflected the state's divided past as the Oklahoma and Indian Territories.

Although Navarre Scott Momaday spent his first year of life at his grandparents' house on the Kiowa Indian reservation in southwestern Oklahoma, his parents, Al and Natachee Scott Momaday, moved to Arizona shortly thereafter to teach on a Navajo reservation, gaining work through the Bureau of Indian Affairs during the Great Depression. Finding teaching a migrant affair, Momaday's parents soon left to teach on two different Apache reservations before finally settling in New Mexico's Rio Grande Valley where they lived and worked at the Pueblo of Jemez. While these experiences lent the future poet a "Pan-Indian experience" that exposed him to a variety of different tribal cultures, his mother made sure that he received a bicultural education in order for him to embrace all parts of his heritage. Subsequently, English was his first language and Kiowa was his second, allowing him easy movement between the Indian world and the white man's world throughout his life.

Because of his parents' constant moving, Momaday went to many different reservation, public, and mission schools. He attended four different high schools as a teenager before relocating to a military academy in Virginia's Shenandoah Valley for his senior year. Here, he hoped to receive adequate college preparation while experiencing the Old South, a region where his mother's Cherokee and white ancestors once lived. After receiving a Bachelor of Arts degree from the University of New Mexico, he taught on the Jicarilla, Apache reservation in Dulce, New Mexico, for a year when he won a poetry fellowship at Stanford University, the only one awarded in 1959, chosen by poet and critic Ivor Winters. Momaday ended up staying in California for twenty years, earning his Ph.D. in literature from Stanford in 1963. During his time at university, he was mentored by Winters, who helped instill in him the importance of order, restraint, and morality in his verse. For his dissertation, Momaday put together a critical edition of poems by Frederick Goddard Tuckerman, a 19th Century poet from New England who depicted nature's minutiae in sonnet form, the subject matter being of great interest to Momaday. This edition, with a forward by Winters, was published as a book by Oxford University Press in 1965. While the book met with critical praise, it failed to raise Tuckerman's canonical stock in academe.

Finding himself overqualified now for reservation teaching, Momaday accepted a position at The University of California at Santa Barbara, where he began focusing on his own creative writing. In 1968, his first novel, *House Made of Dawn*, appeared and was awarded the Pulitzer Prize for fiction the following year. While the popular and critical success of this work allowed Momaday to move to the more prestigious University of California at Berkeley—where he taught English and comparative literature courses and founded a new graduate program in Indian Studies—he found that such quick recognition inhibited him creatively since he was pigeonholed as a novelist. Although many readers still perceive him as such, Momaday considers himself first and foremost a poet, one who intimately explores the Kiowa oral tradition—as well as family and tribe history —while expressing a concern for the environment. As he states, poetry, it seems to me and I'm pretty sure I'm right about this, is the crown of literature. To write a great poem is to do as much as you can do in literature. Everything has to be very precise. The poem has to be informed with motive and emotion. You're bringing everything that literature is based upon to bear, when you write a poem. I think of myself as a poet[.] I'd rather be a poet than a novelist or some other sort of writer. I think I'm more recognized as a novelist, simply because I won a prize. But I write poetry consistently, though slowly.

Because of the time it takes Momaday to write verse, his first book of poetry, *Angle of Geese and Other Poems*, did not appear until 1974 but was quickly followed two years later by *The Gourd Dancer* (1976), the name of which derived from Momaday being named to the Kiowa Gourd Dance Society, an ancient fraternal organization for which he returns to Oklahoma for meetings and dances every summer.

By the mid-1970s, Momaday moved back to his alma mater, Stanford University, where he taught until 1982. During this time, he began experimenting with different literary genres and artistic mediums, writing essays, memoirs, plays, and children's stories and following in his father's footsteps as a painter and visual artist. Subsequently, many of his books include his own artwork, providing visual representations of what he depicts linguistically. His best known book since *House Made of Dawn* is *The Way to Rainy Mountain*, which was published in 1976. In it, he depicts his family and tribe's history in southwestern Oklahoma, using Rainy Mountain as a symbol of his people's historical persistence and connection with the land. A family affair, the book's illustrations were provided by his father, Al.

Since 1982, Momaday has lived in Tucson, teaching at The University of Arizona. He still writes prolifically, often fusing genres in his most recent books. A good example is *In the Bear's House* (2010), where Momaday uses poems, stories, and dialogues to express the spirit of the bear that inhabits his body. In the book's introduction, Momaday writes that

[m]y name is Tsoai-talee, which in Kiowa means "Rock-tree boy." Tsoai, "Rocktree," is Devil's Tower in Wyoming. That is where, long ago, a Kiowa boy

turned into a bear and where his sisters were borne into the sky and became the stars of the Big Dipper. From the time the name Tsoai-talee was conferred on me as an infant, I have been possessed of Bear's spirit [. . .] Bear is the animal representation of the wilderness [. . .] Something in me hungers for wild mountains and rivers and plains.

Momaday's connection to the animal world is expressed best in the poem "To an Aged Bear," where an old bear returns home to die, waiting to "translate" his "spirit" back to nature. Here, the poet urges the bear to "Keep to the trees and waters / Be singing of the soil" to bring himself safely home to the spirit world.

In many ways, "To an Aged Bear" represents Momaday's thoughts and feelings as he approaches the end of his material life. Throughout his eighty years, he has attempted to live by the warrior code of the Plains Indians, who believed in the principles of bravery, fortitude, generosity, and virtue. Expressing these principles in his writing is what makes Momaday an important voice in contemporary American literature. His honorable approach to life and work is surely what attracts readers and is responsible for the many awards and honors he has received, which include being awarded the National Medal of Arts by President George W. Bush in 2007 and earning the Premio Letterario Internazionale "Mondello" in Italy, that country's highest literary honor.

Selected Bibliography

Primary Works

Momaday, N. Scott. *Again the Far Morning: New and Selected Poems.* Albuquerque: U of New Mexico P, 2013.

————. *The Ancient Child: A Novel.* New York: Doubleday, 1989.

————. *Angle of Geese and Other Poems.* Boston: Godine, 1974.

————. *Circle of Wonder: A Native American Christmas Story.* Albuquerque: U of New Mexico P, 1999.

————. *The Gourd Dancer: Poems.* New York: Harper Collins, 1976.

————. *House Made of Dawn.* New York: Harper and Row, 1968.

————. *In the Bear's House.* Albuquerque: U of New Mexico P, 2010.

————. *In the Presence of the Sun: Stories and Poems, 1961–1991.* Albuquerque: U of New Mexico P, 2009.

————. *The Journey of Tai-me.* Albuquerque: U of New Mexico P, 2009.

————. *The Man Made of Words: Essays, Stories, Passages.* New York: St. Martin's, 1997.

————. *The Names: A Memior.* Tucson: U of Arizona P, 1976.

————. *Three Plays: The Indolent Boys, Children of the Sun, and The Moon in Two Windows.* Norman: U of Oklahoma P, 2007.

————. *The Way to Rainy Mountain.* Albuquerque: U of New Mexico P, 1976.

Momaday, N. Scott, ed. *The Complete Poems of Frederick Goddard Tuckerman.* New York: Oxford UP, 1965.

Secondary Works

Clements, William M. "'Image and Word Cannot Be Divided': N. Scott Momaday and Kiowa Ekphrasis." *Western American Literature* 36, no. 2 (2001): 134–52.

Davis, Randall C. "'Something Other and Irresistible and Wild': Bear in the Work of N. Scott Momaday." *JAISA: The Journal of the Association for the Interdisciplinary Study of the Arts* 1, no. 2 (1996): 79–87.

Lincoln, Kenneth. "N. Scott Momaday: Word Bearer." *American Indian Culture and Research Journal* 33, no. 2 (2009): 89–102.

Morgan, Phyllis S. *N. Scott Momaday: Remembering Ancestors, Earth, and Traditions, An Annotated Bio-bibliography*. Norman: U of Oklahoma P, 2010.

"N. Scott Momaday, Ph.D." *Academy of Achievement.* Jan. 23, 2008. <http://www.achievement.org/autodoc/page/momobio-1>. Accessed Dec. 3, 2013.

Roemer, Kenneth M. *Approaches to Teaching Momaday's The Way to Rainy Mountain*. New York: Modern Language Association, 1988.

Schubnell, Matthias. *Conversations with N. Scott Momaday*. Jackson: U of Mississippi P, 1997.

———. *N. Scott Momaday: The Cultural and Literary Background*. Norman: U of Oklahoma P, 1986.

Velie, Alan R. *Four Indian Literary Masters: N. Scott Momaday, James Welch, Leslie Marmon Silko, and Gerald Vizenor*. Norman: U of Oklahoma P, 1982.

Woodard, Charles L. *Conversations with N. Scott Momaday*. Lincoln: U of Nebraska P, 1991.

Selected Poems by N. Scott Momaday

Four Notions of Love and Marriage

For Judith and Richardson Morse, their wedding

1

Formerly I thought of you twice,
as it were.
Presently I think of you once
and for all.

2

I wish you well:
that you are the runners of a wild vine,
that you are the roan and russet of dusk,
that you are a hawk and the hawk's shadow,
that you are grown old in love and delight,
I wish you well.

3

Be still, lovers.
When the moon falls away westward,
there is your story in the stars.

4

In my regalia,
in moccasins,
with gourd and eagle-feather fan,
in my regalia
imagine me;
imagine that I sing
and dance at your wedding.

Plainview

There in the hollow of the hills I see,
Eleven magpies stand away from me.

Low light upon the rim; a wind informs
This distance with a gathering of storms

And drifts in silver crescents on the grass,
Configurations that appear, and pass.

There falls a final shadow on the glare,
A stillness on the dark, erratic air.

I do not hear the longer wind that lows
Among the magpies. Silences disclose,

Until no rhythms of unrest remain,
Eleven magpies standing on the plain.

They are illusion—wind and rain revolve—
And they recede in darkness, and dissolve.

Sun Dance Shield

Mine is a dangerous shield;
there is anger in it,
there is boasting in it.

Mine is a beautiful shield;
there is yellow pollen in it,
there is red earth in it.

Mine is a sacred shield;
there is vision in it,
there is remembrance in it.

Mine is a powerful shield;
there is medicine in it,
there is a sun dance in it.

My life is in this shield,
my life is in this shield.

The Wound

The wound gaped open;
it was remarkably like the wedge of an orange
when it is split, spurting.

He wanted to close the wound with a kiss,
to graft his mouth to the warm, wet tissue.
He kept about the wound, waiting
and deeply disturbed,
his fascination
like the inside of the wound itself,
deep, as deep almost as the life principle,
the irresistible force of being.
The force lay there in the rupture of the flesh,
there in the center of the wound.

Had he been God,
he should himself have inflicted the wound;
and he should have taken the wound gently,
gently in his hands, and placed it
among the most brilliant wildflowers
in the meadows of the mountains.

Fort Sill
Set-angia

You were riding in a wagon to the train.
A tree took shape in the distance.

You began to sing; it was more than unseemly.
The words of your song were so powerful
That nothing less than death could contain them.

At times, many years later, I hear the song,
Not as it was, but as it sounds across time.

Oh my warrior! I love you to sing!
The rattle of your breath, rising to the sun,
I hear among the screams of the hunting horses.

Scaffold Bear

Bears love the taste of whiskey.

—Esther Nahgahnub, 1983

Here in this cave of sleep
I know of an animal on the slope;
No one has seen it,
But there are stories.
Juan Reyes dreamed of it too.
It reared against a moonlit cloud
And sundered the dream.
A young girl spoke of it with wonder,
Having heard it scoop the river for its food.

My own story is this:
A good man killed himself.
The next morning a bear, stripped of its hide,
Lay on a scaffold in a range of trees,
Bleeding, breathing faintly.
Its great paws had been removed.
The bear spoke to someone there, perhaps to me.
For in this cave of sleep,
I am at home to bears.

The Blind Astrologer

Now, at evening, we hear them.
They sheer and shuffle, cracking
branches and heaving the air.
Always shyly they appear.

In radiance they take shape
faintly, their great heads hung low
on arcs of age, their dull eyes
compassing the murky moon.

They sway and impress the earth
with claws. They incise the ice.
Stars of the first magnitude
pulse the making of their dance.

They ascend the ancient bridge
and lay fishes in our way,
so to feed us and our dogs.
Along the green slant southward

the blind astrologers blaze
the long traces of our quest.
They lead us, dead reckoning
by the suns they cannot see.

We regard them with wonder,
fear, and sorrow. They mutter
and cry with voices like ours;
they mime a human anguish.

When they take their leave they fade
through planes and prisms of rain
into the drifts of story,
into calendars and names.

To An Aged Bear

Hold hard this infirmity.
It defines you. You are old.

Now fix yourself in summer,
In thickets of ripe berries,

And venture toward the ridge
Where you were born. Await there

The setting sun. Be alive
To that old conflagration

One more time. Mortality
Is your shadow and your shade.

Translate yourself to spirit;
Be present on your journey.

Keep to the trees and waters.
Be singing of the soil.

Carnegie, Oklahoma, 1919

This afternoon is older
than the giving of gifts
and the rhythmic scraping of the red earth.
My father's father's name is called.
and the gift horse stutters out, whole,
the whole horizon in its eyes.
In the giveaway is beaded
the blood memories of fathers and sons.
Oh, there is nothing like this afternoon
in all the miles and years around,
and I am not here,
but, grandfather, father, I am here.

2009–2010

JIM BARNES

Jim Barnes, Oklahoma's seventeenth poet laureate and the third consecutive Ph.D. named to the position, was born in 1933 and raised in LeFlore County near the town of Summerfield.

His father, Austin Oscar Barnes, was a tenant cotton farmer who transported lumber for a sawmill during the winter months, while his mother, Bessie Vernon Adams Barnes, raised the couple's five children and gardened in her spare time to help make ends meet. Because the Barnes family experienced many lean years, they moved around Summerfield often, looking for a better life that never came. While the family's poor economic situation and the poet's Choctaw and Welsh heritages play important roles in Barnes's work, the most significant event that colored his outlook on life was growing up during World War II, a rupture that brought with it the constant fear of chaos, loss, and death that the poet still feels today. As he relates in his memoir *On Native Ground* (1997),

> [k]illed in battle, lost at sea, missing in action were terms that became commonplace in our lives. We lived with a deepening sense of loss and fear for my brother, Haskell, and my brothers-in-law, Athel Billings and Chester Hamner, and their close encounters with death. Surrounded by the atmosphere of fear and loss, we tried daily to live a normal life, to do things we had to do to keep well and sane [. . .]. Young as I was, I

knew that fate and the world at war cared not a whit
for what we suffered.

Although Barnes rails against what he calls poetry of self-
absorption, his work is at its best when he explores this rural world of
his childhood in eastern Oklahoma, a setting that lends emotional
depth to his poetry that is on par with such confessional poets as
John Berryman (to whom Barnes often alludes) and Robert Lowell.
However, the irony of disapproving of confessional writing while
practicing it seems lost on him. He condemns what he does.

It was as a child that Jim Barnes first fell in love with books. Since
there wasn't much recreational entertainment around Summerfield,
he spent a lot of time reading, which lent him a mental and emotional
escape from the hot summers and cold winters of Oklahoma. Reading
became even more important to him during high school, four years
that he viewed as a complete "waste" since he was "taught nothing.
Neither the love of art, nor the way of the world, nor the worth of
numbers, nor the will to achieve." Only through books did he find
truths about negotiating the struggles of life that lay ahead. Books
also made him want to write: "[i]t was reading, nothing else, that
ultimately made me want to write. Nothing in the blood or the genes
or the culture of eastern Oklahoma made me want to become a
writer." Thus, when he graduated from high school in 1951, he
immediately left for the Pacific Northwest, escaping from a place
that he believed held no cultural value, an opinion that would
eventually change.

Upon arriving in Oregon, where his brother Haskell and sister
Marveda had resettled, Barnes first found work in construction,
helping to build the Lowell Dam, and then as a lumberjack, cutting
trees. Although both of these occupations required strenuous manual
labor, they did afford him time to read during the evenings and
weekends when he wasn't out partying or getting drunk. Growing
tired of being an unskilled laborer, Barnes left Oregon in 1959 and
headed back to Oklahoma, enrolling in Southeastern State College in
Durant in the fall of 1960 to triple major in English, French, and
drama. Here, he found mentors, such as Dennis Letts, who would
foster his dream of becoming a writer.

After graduating from Southeastern in 1964, Barnes married
classmate Cora FloDell McKown. They stayed married for nine years
while both completed graduate school. Barnes ended up earning an
M.A. and a Ph.D. in Comparative Literature from the University of

Arkansas in Fayetteville and taught at Northeastern State College in Tahlequah before finding a permanent position in 1970 at Truman State University in Kirksville, Missouri, where he spent the next thirty three years teaching English, French, and world literature in translation. It was here that he met his second wife, Carolyn Louise Ahlborn. They married in 1973 and stayed together until her death in May 2004.

Although Barnes had been writing short fiction since the mid-1950s and poems since the 1960s, he found little publishing success until the 1970s. In 1978, he was awarded a National Endowment for the Arts Fellowship in Poetry that helped him compose his first book, *This Crazy Land* (1980), which Porch Press published in 1980 when he was forty seven years old. Not wanting to waste any more time, Barnes spent the next three decades publishing seven more books of poetry, a memoir, a book of comparative criticism on Thomas Mann and Malcolm Lowry, and two volumes of translations by poet Dagmar Nick. During this time, he also served as editor of *The Chariton Review*, a literary journal he founded in 1975 to promote his critical antagonism toward confessional writing.

While Barnes's most recent books of poetry, *Paris* (1997) and *Visiting Picasso* (2007), deal with European figures and settings that he encountered while on a number of different poetry fellowships, they lack the intense understanding of foreign cultures needed to be considered major works. Touristy in nature, the poems need the emotional depth of his earlier work, most of which centers on his youth in eastern Oklahoma. Thus, his most important books, *The American Book of the Dead* (1982) and *The Sawdust War* (1992), explore "the horror of utter dissolution" that Barnes feared as a child growing up during World War II. In both books, Barnes positions his personal history inside the larger context of world history, writing about his own experiences with death while hearing about the passing of Hitler, Hirohito, and the victims of Hiroshima. These poems, then, continue his life-long fascination with mortality. This theme finds its way into much of his work, especially poems about the fauna of LeFlore County and local figures and events. One of Barnes's best poems is "An Ex-Deputy Sheriff Remembers the Eastern Oklahoma Murders" from *The American Book of the Dead*. Here, the poet relays the death of four men in the voice of a deputy sheriff who presents events as just another day on the job. Barnes's use of four different narratives— about a Wyoming man beaten to death, a Choctaw shot to death by a police firing squad, a deaf boy run over by an automobile, and a robber shot by a bank manager—shows the variety of ways in which people may die.

Although Jim Barnes was surrounded by an atmosphere of death as a child, he rarely experienced loss in a personal way until 2004 when his wife Carolyn passed away in a car wreck caused by the poet driving off the road after hitting a soft shoulder. Although he had feared such an event throughout his life, he admits that "to have survived [. . .] and not to have the ability to grieve at the time is a burden no one can bear easily." Ironically, he was in too much pain from his crushed ribs and collapsed lungs to have the "energy to grieve." Having retired from Truman State to accept a position at Brigham Young the previous year left Barnes feeling lost and dislocated until fate stepped in and offered him a life-line. As he relates in *On Native Ground,*

> on Christmas day, as I was standing at my kitchen counter trying to decide where to go to have dinner and not be conspicuous, the phone rang. I picked it up and the voice said, "This is Kandi." My response was "Kandi, who?" I was thinking of students, or not thinking at all most likely. The voice replied, "the Kandi you were once married to for nine years!"

After reconnecting, the couple remarried on January 1st, 2006, on the campus of Southeastern Oklahoma State University, where they first met. This event showed Barnes that life carries on. No doubt, his new marriage allowed him to return to European themes in his most recent book, *Visiting Picasso* (2007).

Now in his eighties, Jim Barnes splits his time between Kandi's house in Santa Fe, New Mexico, and his family's ranch in Atoka, Oklahoma, having retired from teaching at Brigham Young in 2006. However, he still remains active on the literary scene by writing and serving as poetry editor at Truman State University Press. Although he has earned many awards and honors during his writing career— including the Oklahoma Book Award in Poetry for *The Sawdust War* and an American Book Award for *On Native Ground*—the honor he most surely treasures was being named the seventeenth poet laureate of his home state, a capstone event to his life that started on a poor farm in LeFlore County. Although he spent much time fearing loss, he rarely imagined how much he could gain.

Selected Bibliography

Primary Works
Barnes, Jim. *The American Book of the Dead*. Urbana: U of Illinois P, 1982.

———. *The Fiction of Malcolm Lowry and Thomas Mann: Structural Tradition*. Kirksville, MO: Thomas Jefferson UP, 1990.

———. *The Fish on Poteau Mountain*. DeKalb, IL: Cedar Creek, 1980.

———. *La Plata Cantata*. West Lafayette, IN: Purdue UP, 1989.

———. *On a Wing of the Sun*. Urbana: U of Illinois P, 2001.

———. *On Native Ground: Memoirs and Impressions*. 1997. Norman: U of Oklahoma P, 2009.

———. *Paris*. Urbana: U of Illinois P, 1997.

———. *The Sawdust War*. Urbana: U of Illinois P, 1992.

———. *A Season of Loss*. West Lafayette, IN: Purdue UP, 1985.

———. *This Crazy Land*. Flagstaff: Porch, 1980.

———. *Visiting Picasso*. Urbana: U of Illinois P, 2007.

———. "Who We Are and What We Do." *American Indian Culture and Research Journal* 35, no. 1 (2011): 67–70.

Barnes, Jim, and Anthony Shelbourne, eds. *Lost Rivers: An Anthology of Native American Poetry*. Guildford, UK: Making Waves, 1997.

Secondary Works

Bataille, Gretchen. "A *Melus* Interview: Jim Barnes." *MELUS* 10, no. 4 (1983): 57–64.

Hedgpeth, Steven. "Bi-Racial Perspective: A Conversation with Jim Barnes." *Pembroke Magazine* 29 (1997): 216–24.

"Jim Barnes." <http://www.jimbarnes.org/>. Accessed December 12, 2013.

Lee, A. Robert, ed. *The Salt Companion to Jim Barnes.* Cambridge, UK: Salt, 2010.

Maio, Samuel. "Memoirs of the Sawdust Generation." *Paintbrush: A Journal of Contemporary Multicultural Literature* 19 (1992): 29–34.

Rodriguez, Linda. "Contemporary Profile: Jim Barnes." *Potpourri*, May 4, 1994, 3.

Woehik, Heinz. "An Interview with Jim Barnes." *Paintbrush: A Journal of Contemporary Multicultural Literature* 13 (1986): 52–61.

Selected Poems by Jim Barnes

Skipping

Something never quite returns when you want
the facts the way you'd like the past to be.
It was our last day together: the sun
was bright, the new grass up, the water right,
and no one cared that we had missed the day.

You can't quite remember getting there, or
which of you did this or that: skipping stones
was in our blood. This was our vague good-bye,
a salute to the world of the narrow stream
we frolicked in and the school two miles away.

You never get it right without the weather:
the May sun warmed our cheeks. We swam till noon.
Then the girls spread lunch on the bank under
the sycamore tree. Above us the Tarzan swing
was a thread of the sun, and we drifted

on a wave of small thought and talk, already
forgetting what we had been those walled years.
But still it's not quite right: you remember
more than was. The love didn't really happen.
You were too shy, or the others were wrapped

up in future selves. You knew that someone
almost drowned: two others pulled him out by
the hair. He'd dived too deep. There was a knot
on his crown. Or maybe he'd just faked it
for the tears the girls almost didn't shed.

What is this life? We should have asked stones,
grass, stream. We idled down the sun. The songs
we sang should have echoed off whatever
doom or dance we still beat time to. But they
fade, and the faces come up wrong, the facts

a reconstruction of no consequence. Once
you've done it, you never lose the knack of
skipping flat stones. How smooth the rock feels
against thumb and fingers as you release it
into its final spin and brief buoyancy.

An Ex-Deputy Sheriff Remembers
the Eastern Oklahoma Murders

Summerfield

They took a tire tool to his head,
this gentle stranger from Wyoming.
Oh, we caught them over
at Talihina drinking beer
at Lester's Place, calling
the myna bird bad names
and shooting shuffleboard.
I'm telling you
they were meek in the muzzle
of our guns. They claimed innocence
and: why, they went fishing
with the Cowboy just the other day.
We said we knew, knew too
the way they stole him blind
that night. We spoke of blood,
the way the dogs had lapped his face.
The youngest of the three bad brothers,
barely thirteen, began to cry:
"He told us everything was all right
and we hit him till he died."
And that is how it was,
a simple thing, like breathing,
they hit him until he died,
until he bled Wyoming dry
there on the road
in that part of Oklahoma
no stranger has ever owned.

Red Oak

We shot the Choctaw way back in '94,
last legal execution by firing squad.
He didn't die, through the heart, square
and he didn't die.
The high sheriff, my old boss,
stuffed his own shirt down
the Choctaw's neck

to stop the rattle in his throat.
You couldn't shoot a downed man
no matter what and he had to die.
Damned good Choctaw, I'll say that.
Red Oak had no jail and it was too
blasted cruel to execute him
before his crop was in. The judge
scheduled it for the fall, first Saturday
after the corn was in the Choctaw's crib.
That damned fool Choctaw gathered
his corn like any other dirt farmer,
dressed clean, and kept his word.
"I'm ready" is all he said that day.
You got to admire a man like that,
Indian or not, murderer or just plain fool.
He'd shot three men for sleeping
in his barn and taking the milk bucket
away from his little girl, though she
wasn't harmed at all, and he showed up
just like he'd said he would.

                       There
was a picnic in the shade after we choked
the Choctaw to death and took the rifle home.
First time I'd ever seen a camera,
big damned black thing on legs,
smelled like seven kinds of sin every time
it popped. Had fresh hominy and chicken and the last
of some damned fine late sweet red watermelons.

Leflore
Goddamnest thing I ever saw
was when old Mac ran down that poor old LeFlore boy.
Old Mac was drunk as thunder
when we chained him to the tree
he'd just pissed on back of his house.
Said he'd wanted to see what it was like
to bounce a man off the hood

of the truck he hauled pulpwood on.
No other reason than just that.
Hell of a note, but I've heard worse.
They all have got some sort of song and dance.
Old Mac's kids were screaming louder
than the crows and threatening us with gardening hoes.
We shooed them off with fake fast draws.
That poor old LeFlore boy was deaf as a stone,
a condition they say came with the color of his skin,
though as mild in his ways as the first fall winds.
Old Mac had hit him from behind. Coming
down the gravel road, lord, he must have been
doing sixty and with a full two-cord load.
Hit him dead on. Center. Cracked his
back in half all the way through. That poor
old LeFlore boy's rubber boots were
left standing exactly where he last had stood.
How can you account for that, those silly
rubber boots standing bolt upright
dead in the middle of the goddamned road?

Wister

What made him think he could get away with it
is beyond me. Hell, he'd lived over at Glendale
all his life. Everybody knew he had a stiff
little finger on his right hand. The mask hid
nothing, not even the fear and tobacco juice
he always drooled out the corners of his mouth.
He shot the teller right between the eyes and
made the others strip. Don't ask why. Cleaned
out the vault of a thousand dollars, mostly
fives, and made it fifty yards down the Frisco
tracks before Mathes, the bank's owner, naked
as a jaybird and pissing a blue streak, blew
his left shoulder off with a 30.06. I've got
the cartridge shell to this day. Was going to
have one of them little lighters, size of your
finger, made out of it. But I decided to quit.

The Heavener Runes

Old words vague
as reeds on water.

Gouged runes
cold as glaciers.

Who can tell
a thought
from stone?
Only the glyph
speaks.
Thought is lost.

The thing itself
remains.

Hot earth.
Cold sky.
You between.

To make a mark
you become the mark.
Your name.
A woman's.
The date.

It does not matter:
you are the mark,
you are the stone.

JIM BARNES

Hogging Below the Gates at Wister Dam

In spring flood time the Corps of Engineers
opened the gates to let the water level
down, and the exiled bass, bream, catfish, and drum,
rushed the sluice in such numbers you could feel
them brush your legs. I came at night to wade
the rapids, hogging any fish I caught
into gunnysacks. I was too crazy
for fish to let them pass upstream to their
lost homes and rut among the dark drowned leaves.

What mattered then was innocence and guilt,
of which the fish knew nothing. I watched
old men daily take their limit of bass
or bluegill or channel cat. I knew it
was wrong in the game warden's eyes to hog
when only one hook per line was allowed.
I knew it was wrong the old men took fish
for the sake of eggs alone. I forgot moral
things as the sun went down and the moon said go.

What matters now is much the same, except
the fish are gone, have been gone these forty
years, the cycle cut by dam and hogging boys
and old men mad for the taste of fresh fish eggs.
Now you can wade the Poteau anywhere
below the dam and never feel a fin
or scales brush your legs. Few fish are drifting
here. The water is docile even in flood,
and the moon has no voice, and the fish no home.

After the Great Plains

Nothing remains the same in this long land.
Bird, fox, gully, grass, all are history
as soon as the moon rises or the wind climbs,
tales told by shadows leaning toward a vista
few eyes discern.

What strikes the windshield hardest as you drive
across is haze, distance claiming being
as absolute as the grasshoppers crushed on
the glass. There is no sameness to a land
that paints itself

different each dawn. The wind in your hair
today becomes a mouse's breath four states
beyond tomorrow. The river you ford could not
be any river. Particular, it flows through
the heart of the land.

After the Great Plains you are not the same.
No matter which way you cross something stays
firmly with you, a sense hard to name, like
a pebble in the toe of your boot you can't shake
out in this life.

2011–2012

EDDIE D. WILCOXEN

In December 2010, just as he was leaving office, Governor Brad Henry appointed Eddie Wilcoxen as Oklahoma's eighteenth poet laureate, a choice that was not without controversy among writers and educators in the state. While his four immediate predecessors were college professors, three of whom held Ph.D. degrees, Wilcoxen was a community college graduate best known as a radio broadcaster and martial arts expert. While some harbored hard feelings about his appointment, Wilcoxen fits in with such earlier laureates as Delbert Davis and Joe Kreger by writing poetry for a mass audience, representing Oklahoma's folksy, non-elitist citizenry. Like them, his work is for all to enjoy, breaking the recent tradition of choosing sophisticated, well-educated poets to the position. Wilcoxen's dedication to poetry and civic engagement also made him one of the state's most active laureates. During his tenure, he made more than one hundred appearances and readings, illustrating that he is, indeed, a poet of the people.

Not originally an Oklahoman, Wilcoxen lived in Kansas, Colorado, New Mexico, Virginia, and Ohio before settling in Altus in the early 1980s, where he has lived ever since. He was raised on a farm just south of Dodge City, Kansas, one of six boys born to Kenneth and Ruby Wilcoxen. Although his brothers helped with the farm work, Eddie suffered from a number of illnesses, including polio and severe asthma, which kept him in hospitals for half of his childhood. It was during his hospital stays that he first developed a love for poetry, listening to his mother read to him as he lay bedridden. These illnesses, as well as his partial paralysis from polio, lent him a grit and determination that helped him to thrive as an adult both personally and professionally.

After graduating from Dodge City Community College in 1969, Wilcoxen briefly attended Kansas University before transferring to the Radio Engineering Institute of Kansas City, where he earned his first Phone Engineering License from the Federal Communications Commission (FCC). This began his professional radio career on KWHW in Altus. Determined not to let his physical disability impair him, Wilcoxen also began studying martial arts at this time, eventually becoming a three time National Karate Champion. Because of this achievement, he was chosen to carry the Olympic torch on its journey to Atlanta for the 1996 games, one of the highlights of his life.

It was as a child that Wilcoxen began writing poetry—he put together his first collection of poems in second grade as a present to his mother for Valentine's Day. Although he continued this practice into adulthood, he didn't take writing seriously until his wife Joan encouraged him to share his poems with the public when he was well into middle-age. With her help, he founded CTK Publishing, which has issued eleven of his poetry books, most of which are thematic collections that include *Oklahoma Proud!: A Centennial Book of Poems* (2007), *Reflections of a Wandering Mind* (2009), and *Rose Petal Poems— Tales of Life and Love* (2013). He was named poet laureate after Altus's public library and the town's local humanities organization nominated him.

The best example of Wilcoxen's work is *Oklahoma Proud!*, the volume in which he celebrates the towns, landscape, and people of Oklahoma in verse written in either four-line stanzas or rhymed couplets. Published to coincide with the state's centennial, the book documents the "wonderful solid values and warm and friendly culture of Oklahoma." While many of Wilcoxen's poems express sentimentality over certain places or admiration for particular historical figures, all show his love for his adopted state and its tough-minded citizens. Like most laureates since the mid-1990s, Wilcoxen also composed a piece about the 1995 bombing of the Alfred P. Murrah Building. Entitled "Oklahoma City Memorial," the poem depicts the good that can grow out of evil, which occurred

immediately after the terrorist act when fellow Americans began
offering aid to their Oklahoma brethren:

Crises is the crucible where character is forged and found,
and the people of Oklahoma stood tall and held their ground.

They put aside their tears and did the work they had to face,
and felt the soothing comfort of a nation's warm embrace.

From all across America, the prayers and people poured,
to help Oklahoma—to help beat back the sword.

Such end-stopped, rhyming lines and sentimental, patriotic
themes are typical of Wicoxen's verse. As such, they are easy to relate
to and understand by everyone, specialists and lay-readers alike.

Although his tenure as Oklahoma's poet laureate ended in 2012,
Eddie Wilcoxen remains active in the arts within the state. In 2014,
he and his wife Joan were elected to a two year term as Co-Presidents
of the Poetry Society of Oklahoma, which was founded in 1934 to
strengthen and expand poetry in areas outside of academe. The
couple's goals in the position include establishing local poetry
chapters state-wide, increasing youth involvement with the
organization, and establishing more adult mentors for young writers.
As Wilcoxen told the *Altus Times* newspaper about his appointment:
"As the Official State Poet, I got to talk with hundreds of people. One
of the things that became clear is that poetry is misunderstood. It's
deemed by most to be the province of English teachers and
Professors [sic]. We've allowed the voice of every day Oklahoma to be
silenced in favor of some academic ideal of what poetry should be."
To change this, Wilcoxen maintains a youtube channel, entitled
"eddiestuff," where videos featuring his reading of poems can be
found. These clips show that his work is made up of performance
pieces that are better heard orally than read silently. Wilcoxen's
appointment as Co-President to the Poetry Society of Oklahoma
ensures that he will remain active in the state's poetry scene for years
to come, making poetry more accessible to all citizens within the
state.

Selected Bibliography

Primary Works

Wilcoxen, Eddie D. *Oklahoma Proud!: A Centennial Book of Poems.* Altus, OK: CTK Publishing, 2007.

————. *Reflections of a Wandering Mind.* Altus, OK: CTK Publishing, 2009.

————. *Rose Petal Poems—Tales of Life and Love.* Altus, OK: CTK Publishing, 2013.

Secondary Works

"Altus Man appointed Oklahoma Poet Laureate." kwso.com. January 19, 2011. <http://www.kswo.com/story/13871892/altus-man-appointed-next-oklahoma-poet-laureate>. Accessed January 13, 2014.

"A Man of Many Talents." okmag.com. September 2011. <http://www.okmag.com/September-2011/A-Man-Of-Many-Talents/>. Accessed January 13, 2014.

"Poetry by Eddie D. Wilcoxen." 2008. <http://www.eddiestuff.com/>. Accessed February 11, 2014.

"Wilcoxens chosen as Co-Presidents for Poetry Society of Oklahoma." http://altustimes.com/news/news/2673916/Wilcoxens-chosen-as-Co-Presidents-for-Poetry-Society-of-Oklahoma. altustimes.com.

Selected Poems by Eddie Wilcoxen

Jumping the Cimarron

I've seen the Cimarron a half mile wide
at its conjunction with the Arkansas.
But I've jumped across the Cimarron
and not even wet my feet, down there in the draw.

That was out in the far west reaches
of where the river runs,
before it fills with water spilled
from the land through which it comes.

But we must remember the Cimarron
is called the "river that runs dry."
For many miles in the heat of summer
no water flows on by.

It just puddles here and there—
few signs of glories yet to come,
out in far west Oklahoma,
early on the Cimarron!

Geronimo

GERONIMO, proud Apache chief,
GERONIMO, wild spirit leap,
GERONIMO, man of legend,
GERONIMO, his deeds transcend!

GERONIMO, prisoner of war,
GERONIMO, he paced the floor,
GERONIMO, in old Fort Sill
GERONIMO, his spirit lingers still!

GERONIMO, a famous cry,
GERONIMO WILL NEVER DIE!

Little Prairie Home

Where is the man who built me? Who labored day and night?
Long it's been since he left here, with his children and his wife.

I miss their laughter in the hall, the squeal of children's play;
no more the light of kerosene lamp at the darkened end of day.

I hear no quiet bedtime prayers, no whispered secrets sweet.
Boarded and shuttered and left alone, no one do I meet.

Occasionally through the passing years, as I fall into disrepair,
someone will come and wander here, wondering who it was lived
here?

If only they could hear me! What a tale I'd tell—
of love and sorrow, pleasure and pain, of heaven and hell!

I've seen the bitter struggles, seen tears of joy and pain.
I've heard the sounds of nighttime love, and anguished cries for rain!

Through these broken empty panes, hungry eyes have stared a
thousand times,
wondering about the world beyond this quiet country lane, past all
this work and country grime.

I know it wasn't easy, but the children always ate,
and once I had new paint, a picket fence, and a wooden garden gate.

Through the years, I've lost some shingles, the porch is torn askew.
Nearby, the well is dry, the windmill too ramshackle to ever turn anew.

The swallows nest up in my eaves, the rabbits in the yard.
The trees they planted long ago still linger, but life for them is hard.

The tumbleweeds roll by my door, the coyote howls nearby
and I am empty and alone, as through me night winds sigh.

My time came and went so quickly—happy family here—then gone
to flight.
Little time remains for me, but while I stand, perhaps someone will
see, and then will write.

Will write about the way I sheltered them, kept them safe and warm.
Will tell of my noble efforts to shield them from life's storms.

Perhaps someone will tell of my service—loyal through and through
when this country was first settled and homes were far and few!

Oklahoma City Memorial

In Oklahoma City terror struck—there's no defense for madness!
In the aftermath, emotions boiled. There was anger—there was
sadness.

The who, the why, the questions, spinning in each head,
as the torn and shattered building fell around the many dead.

Crisis is the crucible where character is forged and found,
and the people of Oklahoma stood tall and held their ground.

They put aside their tears and did the work they had to face,
and felt the soothing comfort of a nation's warm embrace.

From all across America, the prayers and people poured,
to help Oklahoma—to help beat back the sword.

A handful of ignorant and evil men wreaked havoc in OKC,
but in the end, grace and goodness triumphed over deaths' decree!

Today there is a memorial where the Murrah Building stood,
a place to mourn the fallen, to remember all things good.

It's a monument to courage, and to the strength of love,
a place where people go to reflect and send prayers to up above!

2013–2014

NATHAN BROWN

After Eddie Wilcoxen's tenure as Oklahoma's poet laureate ended in 2012, Governor Mary Fallin named Nathan Brown to the position, returning to the recent practice of appointing poets with doctorate degrees. Although Brown earned his Ph.D. in Creative and Professional Writing at the University of Oklahoma, he, like Wicoxen, believes in composing and promoting non-academic poetry to the citizens of Oklahoma. As Brown states on his website, brownlines.com: "his mission is to take back poetry from the hard academic ivory tower and those who too often use poetry for personal therapy." Because of this belief, Brown, like his favorite contemporaries Stephen Dunn, Tony Hoagland, Sharon Olds, and Billy Collins, writes intelligent but accessible poetry for a mass audience, hoping to win back readers to verse within the United States.

Born on March 16th, 1965, to a Baptist preacher and his artist wife, Brown refers to himself as a hopeful cynic, one who was raised in the First Baptist Church of Norman but who questions God's handiwork as an adult. Although he is best known as a poet, Brown actually came to verse circuitously through music. By the time he was a teenager, he was working as a professional musician in local bands in southern Oklahoma. In his twenties, he relocated to Nashville to work as a singer/songwriter. This move, however, ended up destroying his love for music in just a few months. Subsequently, he didn't pick up an instrument for approximately five years, turning to other interests outside of music instead.

It was while taking a creative writing course with George Economou at the University of Oklahoma that Brown first became interested in poetry. Unlike the lyrics he had been writing and listening to, he found poetry confusing and complicated. It wasn't until after reading Stephen Dunn's "At the Smithville Methodist Church" that Brown became a poetry convert. As he relates, "I said out loud to myself: If poetry can do that, sign me up," identifying with the poem's negative view of organized religion and Christianity, which many use to exclude others from their social group. From there, Brown never looked back. Eventually, he became so dedicated to verse that he wrote a poem a day for fifteen years straight. Many of these 5,500 poems found their way into his books, the first of which, *Hobson's Choice*, was published by Greystone Press in 2002. Over the next twelve years he published seven additional books of poetry and a memoir. *Two Tables Over* (2008) was awarded the Oklahoma Book Award for poetry in 2009, an unofficial prerequisite for being appointed to the state's poet laureate position.

Even though Brown is prolific, accounting for his quick succession of books, he remains dedicated to the craft of composing poetry, carefully revising his verse before publication. He is also known for the breadth of poems he writes. While he used *Hobson's Choice* to play with the visual field of verse—writing ironical poems and parodies that experimented with font, type size, spacing, and punctuation—his following two books, *Ashes over the Southwest* (2005) and *Suffer the Little Vocies* (2005), are more confessional, containing jeremiads about the negative things religion does to people, problematic relationships with his family, and the hum-drum events of daily life. In his most recent book, *Less is more, more or less* (2013), Brown further expresses his versatility by composing poems that can fit onto a 5 x 7 note card, a forced expression of brevity. As he states, "I've been convinced for a long time now that the world has too many words in it. And it's not just 'too much information.' We also live in an absolute glut of utterly useless, if not worthless, information . . . I believe that well-written poetry, and the power contained in its brevity, is the best antidote to the poison." Although Brown rails against the academic difficulty of Ezra Pound's esoteric work, his latest book shows that he is a firm believer in two of Pound's credos:

"go in fear of abstractions" and "make it new! Day by day, make it new!"

When asked if he could point to one particular poem that best represents his work, Brown could not settle on one but chose two poems instead: the humorous piece "Between Two Artists" from *Suffer the Little Voices* and "The Sign" from *Two Tables Over*. In the former poem, Brown writes an open letter to God, chastising him for his "installation piece / at the Point Lobos Nature Reserve / above Big Sur" that "simply goes too far" by being too perfect to be taken seriously with its tall pines, superimposed cliffs, and crashing waves. The narrator argues that the scene "does not speak to the truth / of the way things are" in the world, ironically criticizing the perfect beauty that gives refuge to imperfect people. In his serious poem "The Sign," Brown depicts a time when he becomes aware of his own stereotyped prejudice, which highlights his personal shortcomings. As the poem opens, the narrator notices a woman with "bleach-blond hair down the back, / blue eyes and too much makeup [. . .]." Having "decided already what this poem / was going to be about [. . .]," his expectations are shattered when he learns that the woman and her father (or her lover) are both deaf. After this realization, he states that "the trusses of my preconceptions / begin to buckle. The edges of prejudice / begin to crumble like dry toast . . . ," symbolized concretely when Brown breaks the form of the last stanza. Not only did this experience remind him that the poet's job is to flout expectations by viewing things in new ways, but it also taught him not to take people at face value since humanity is always complex enough to defy stereotypes. No doubt, he chose this as a representative poem since it serves as a constant reminder to avoid misconceptions and societal expectations.

Although Nathan Brown currently teaches courses in the University of Oklahoma's Liberal Studies Department, he stays busy by giving public readings and creativity workshops as part of his poet laureate appointment while finding time to work as a professional photographer and musician. Depressed by the growing difficulty of publishing poetry in the United States, he founded Mezcalita Press, where he continues his work as a literary "Johnny Appleseed" by writing poems "unafraid of making sense." Because of his out-going nature, his tireless energy, and his poetic accessibility, Nathan Brown has been one of the most popular of Oklahoma's nineteen poets laureate. The current state of verse is surely better off by his presence and dedication.

Selected Bibliography

Primary Works

Brown, Nathan. *Ashes Over the Southwest: Poems*. Edmond, OK: Greystone Press, 2005.

—————. *Hobson's Choice*. Edmond, OK: Greystone Press, 2002.

—————. *Karma Crises: New and Selected Poems*. Norman, OK: Mezcalita Press, 2012.

—————. *Less is more, more or less*. Norman, OK: Mezcalita Press, 2013.

—————. *Letters to the One-Armed Poet*. Cheyenne, OK: Village Books Press, 2011.

—————. *My Sideways Heart*. Norman, OK: Mongrel Empire Press, 2010.

—————. *Nôt Exăctly Jōb*. Norman, OK: Mongrel Empire Press, 2008.

—————. *Suffer the Little Voices*. Edmond, OK: Greystone Press, 2005.

—————. *Two Tables Over*. Cheyenne, OK; Village Books Press, 2008.

Secondary Works

"Nathan Brown—2013/2014 Oklahoma Poet Laureate." <http://brownlines.com/>. Accessed March 4, 2014.

"Nathan Brown Appointed Oklahoma Poet Laureate." Oklahoma Humanities Council. <http://www.okhumanities.org/nathan-brown-appointed-oklahoma-poet-laureate>. Accessed February 18, 2014.

Smith, Erica. "Norman Author's *Letters* Offers a Poignant Look at Friendship that Lives On." Newsok. March 28, 2011. <http://newsok.com/article/3551443>. Accessed March 2, 2014.

Selected Poems by Nathan Brown

Such is Life

The three of them are playing LIFE
when I arrive to pick up my daughter
for our one-day weekend. My ex,
her new hubby, and my little girl

swap orange and green money,
spin the plastic wheel, and move
red, white, and yellow plastic cars
with pink and blue people in them.

My ex constantly checks the rules
on the box lid, as she's always done.

Her husband stares at the floor . . .
refuses Homeowners Insurance.

And my baby girl is married,
has a son, and will probably retire
with a few million dollars.

They argue quite a bit over details,
squabble over taxes . . . and the fact
that my girl chose the ARTIST card.

And I am forced to sit by
and watch
until they are done.

NATHAN BROWN

As the Minister of Propriety and Fermentation

Mom hands me the list—
    hand-written on the back
    of church stationary—
with a wince of hope in her eyes.

    KJ – 2

is code for a couple of nice
Kendall Jackson Chardonnays.
Vintner's Reserve...her favorite.

Then:
    Champagne
    1 Andre Ex. Dry
    1 Beringer pink
            ...if enough money

And she handed that list to me
because she is a preacher's wife—
even if that preacher retired years ago.

And this is just how it's done
here on the plains of Oklahoma.

Liberated as she may be,
a temperate, upstanding woman
married to a Baptist minister

enlists an accomplice—
    someone beyond redemption
        to buy her booze.

Lowland Heretic

Down by the base of a wheat stalk
in the well-tended fields of Lower-
Great-Plains-Republicans, I lie . . .

a brown slithering Democrat,
narrowly escaping the occasional blaze
of buckshot and boot soles at cockfights,
roosters with razor blades.

Once buried in the holy waters
of a good Southern Baptism
at the age of seven,

I now raise
a sinful hand up and out toward
the softly shaking head of St. Jude

in hopes he'll rescue this lonely lost cause
from the rage of a red-faced denomination
that lords an iron-fisted domination
over the souls of good people

who can't see the fat
clogging its veins
and arteries.

Between Two Artists

Dear God,
    I have always admired
your work. And were it not for that,
I wouldn't bother you with this. But,

I must say that your installation piece
at the Point Lobos Nature Reserve
above Big Sur simply goes too far.

The Monterey pines are too tall,
the cypresses too fanned out in perfection
from trunks tied in intricate knots
that would take centuries
to unravel.

                        The cliffs appear
superimposed for dramatic effect
with impossible jags giving way
to fairytale caves that burst forth gushes
of blue water like a French soda topped
with a spray of whipped cream.

The crash of waves and explosions of foam
are too much like a Disneyland ride.
There are too many kinds of birds,
too many varieties of plants,
and too much color in both, I might add.

In short, it lacks integrity.
It does not speak the truth
of the way things are. And I don't think
viewers will trust, or believe,
its authenticity.

Biblical Proportions

When God swings the fist
of weather in Oklahoma,
we pull up seats and lean
into the performance—

here on the stage that gave us
one of the great panoramic visions
of the 20th Century when it comes to
heaven's fit of meteorological rage.

The Dust Bowl, stirred up
by an army of angel wings,
came in like a black tidal wave
of interstellar grit and dirt.

It ground its stained teeth
as it passed over and turned
small homesteads and barns
into dunes and shallow graves.

The few surviving souls
were forced to punch holes
through shingles in the roof
to get a view of the damage.

Heard tell of one old man
who said, *Ol' Noah never
had no troubles like this.
Least he had time to build a boat.*

United States

Except for the thin membrane
of Oklahoma's Panhandle,
Texas and Colorado almost touch.

On a clear day one could almost see
smoke signals from the other
drifting up and over Black Mesa
where jackrabbits jet among sage.

***

There is something of the in-between
in this windblown space where my favorite states
hold hands in tenuous agreement,
　　not quite trusting each other,
　　but trusting "all else" much less.

There is a quiet hill here
that never forgot the Trojan War,
the Fall of Rome, or the Spanish Inquisition,
because it never knew they happened.

There is a small town here,
Boise City, that knows World War II
because in '43 a home team B-17
mistook the courthouse lights
for a test range down the road.

***

Here, where Texas almost touches Colorado
the rocks and stunted trees stand between
states . . .　　between generations . . .
solid among the arms of the Milky Way.

And that's why this place laughed
that day the power-grid shut down
up in New York City. Folks out here
snorted at their panic and shock.

Out here where a moonless night
is so dark, you can't see
the ground beneath your feet.

Remember Los Alamos

Best part's the drive in.
The town itself leaves me
a little dry, like every time
my president utters "nuc-u-lar"
for the type of weapons
everyone else should not have.

I'm sure there's something
at its core, something cool
like winter, or a hot nightlife,
but I can't find it.

I turn right on Oppenheimer Road
hoping something will explode
into view, but it only goes 100 feet,
then dead ends at the public library.

While sippin' heavy coffee in Café Allegro,
a huge Peach Granola Muffin just glows
with flavor like there was a great big buttery
meltdown in the back of the kitchen.

A Japanese family sits two tables over—
two fabulous daughters with fabulous tattoos.

And the bumper sticker on the register reads:

LOS ALAMOS
BIRTHPLACE OF THE BOMB

The Sign

She comes in—tanned, tight jeans,
bleach-blond hair down the back,
blue eyes and too much makeup—

with a baby on her hip. And I'd
decided already what this poem
was going to be about, when she

sits down across from what looks
to be her father and begins to sign
with her one free hand. He smiles

and signs back—hands rolling effusively,
lips moving in a soundless poetry.
Their gazes trade loves back and forth.

The baby's eyes glow in the wave
and trickle of mom's fingers that must
look like birds close enough to touch.

And the trusses of my preconceptions
begin to buckle. The edges of prejudice
begin to crumble like dry toast . . .

and . . .   I have made a mistake.

I want to go over and apologize,
But I don't know the sign for that.

University

I spent 23 good years
and my parents' savings
deboning its favorite texts
for the title and deed
to the grave privilege
of calling a crock
a crock
when I see it
stewing and steaming
before me.

The Villainous Nelle

I held in contempt, yet admired as welle
With utmost respect, I secretly hated
The one who created the villainous nelle

The recurring lines, the tenth syllabelle
Impossible rhymes and meters upended
I held in contempt, yet admired as welle

Its difficult structure, Gematraic helle
In doing my best, I wriggled and wrested
With the one who created the villainous nelle

Plenty of paper, ink's bottomless welle
A poet with plenty of time to be wasted
I held in contempt, yet admired as welle

The lack of TV was easy to telle
In the poetic home of the one whom I hated
The one who created the villainous nelle

They have now padded my artistic celle
From when I combated, cried then decided
I held in contempt, yet admired as welle
The one who created the villainous nelle

2015–2016

BENJAMIN MYERS

On February 24th, 2014, just three days before Thanksgiving, Benjamin Myers received notice from Governor Mary Fallin that he was chosen as Oklahoma's twentieth poet laureate. Myers had been nominated by Audell Shelburne, the English Department chairperson at Northeastern State University in Tahlequah, and by other English faculty members. His term commenced on January 1st, 2015, and will end two years later on December 31st, 2016. Myers' appointment confirmed the recent commitment by Oklahoma's governors of naming the state's most educated poets to the position. Of the last six laureates, starting with Francine Ringold in 2003, five have held doctoral degrees, including Myers, who holds a Ph.D. in Renaissance literature. Appointed as poet laureate at age 39, he is also the second youngest person to serve in the position, coming in second to Paul Kroeger who was appointed at age 24 in 1931.

Upon being born in the town of Chandler on April 25, 1975, Myers was immediately immersed into the heady world of language. His father, Paul Myers, was a minor poet who held poetry workshops and worked odd jobs to make ends meet while his mother, Anna Myers, was a school teacher who eventually became a well-known young adult novelist. As Myers relates, he came to writing because it was "the family business, a natural thing to do." Although he wrote his first serious poem to impress a girl named Mandy Matthews—which must have worked since he married her years later—his need to write eventually grew into an obsession. As he notes, "I tried to quit writing but couldn't." He finally learned to live with his obsession by accepting that poetry is "the thing I do."

Myers' early success with the written word landed him a "full ride scholarship" at the University of the Ozarks in Clarksville, Arkansas, where he naturally majored in English. Two things that drew him to the school was its traditional English Department, where he built a strong foundation in literary history, and its proximity to good hiking trails and lakes for fishing. Although he fell in love with contemporary poetry at this time, especially the work of American and British confessional poets, he ended up writing his Ph.D. dissertation at Washington University in St. Louis on "The Ethical Landscape of Edmund Spencer: Colonial Ecology in the *Faerie Queen.*" He found that focusing on Renaissance literature gave him much needed distance from contemporary poetry. Undoubtedly, this specialization lent his own verse greater breadth in theme, content, and style.

Although Myers still lives in his hometown of Chandler, he teaches at Oklahoma Baptist University in Shawnee, where he serves as the Crouch-Mathis Professor of Literature. He is the author of two books, *Elegy for Trains* (2010), for which he won the Oklahoma Book Award for Poetry in 2011, and *Lapse Americana* (2013), which was published by New York Quarterly Books. Both volumes are highly allusive with epigraphs included by Virgil, Shakespeare, and Woody Guthrie and with poems referencing Lucretius, Li Po, Dante, Ezra Pound, T. S. Eliot, Wallace Stevens, John Berryman, and John Coltrane. Christianity and biblical themes are also prevalent in both. However, while *Elegy for Trains* is typical of many first books by containing short, confessional poems that explore the poet's personal history, Myers made *Lapse Americana* longer, more meditative, and much darker in scope; in this volume, he is especially haunted by his father's death from cancer in 1999. Not only has Myers lengthened his lines and diversified his style, but he also uses *Lapse Americana* to explore the underbelly of American life. The wide array of characters that appear are ones for whom the American Dream has disappeared: criminals, ne'er-do-wells, soldiers, bullies, drunkards, racists, and old men. He even includes a poem about lice. The poetic themes that Myers explores in *Lapse Americana* no doubt helped to attract its major New York publisher. While the book's poems are approachable in both style and content, the majority of them reflect the troubled times during which they were written. A diverse reading audience will find it relevant to their own lives.

Along with his two books, Myers' poems have appeared in a wide array of periodicals and anthologies, including *Byline, Nimrod, Iron Horse Review, The New York Quarterly, The New Plains Review, Plainsongs, Tar River Poetry, The Blue Collar Review, Ain't Nobody that Can Sing Like Me: New Oklahoma Writing,* and *Travelin' Music: A Tribute to Woody Guthrie.* Although he sometimes writes in traditional forms —like earlier poets laureate he is especial to sonnets and villanelles— he is much more interested in exploring "what can be done rather than imposing limits." Thus, free verse allows him the room to find "the possibilities of a poem." He often likes to emulate the verse experiments of John Berryman and Frank O'Hara. This usually manifests itself in Myers attempting to blend a narrative and lyric together in the same poem.

When asked if he was surprised at his appointment as Oklahoma's twentieth poet laureate, he answered, "yes, very surprised." Although initially caught off guard, he, like his predecessor Nathan Brown, anticipates an active two year term. Among his goals are to work with children and high school students to encourage them to read and write poetry. Since he doesn't like to talk much about himself, he also wants to use his platform to promote other great Oklahoma poets, especially Dorothy Alexander and Ken Hada. Above all, he wants to show the general public that "poems are not about finding a hidden message but are, instead, about having pleasure and fun." No doubt, his own poems will go a long way to support his point and will help to further the cause of poetry throughout the state.

Selected Bibliography

Primary Works

Myers, Benjamin. "Ashbery's 'They Dream Only of America' and 'Definition of Blue.'" *Explicator* 65, no. 1 (2006): 47–50.

———. *Elegy for Trains*. Cheyenne, OK: Village Books Press, 2010.

———. "'Following the Way Which is Called Heresy': Milton and the Heretical Imperative." *Journal of the History of Ideas* 69, no. 3 (2008): 375–393.

———. *Lapse Americana*. New York: New York Quarterly Books, 2013.

———. "Milton's Paradise Lost, Book 11." *Explicator* 64, no. 1 (2005): 14–17.

———. "'Such is the Face of Falsehood': Spenserian Theodicy in Ireland." *Studies in Philology* 103, no. 4, (2006): 383–416.

Myers, Benjamin P. "The Green and Golden World: Spenser's Rewriting of the Munster Plantation." *ELH* 76, no. 2 (2009): 473–490.

———. "Pro-War and Prothalamion: Queen, Colony, and Somatic Metaphor among Spenser's 'Knights of the Maidenhead.'" *English Literary Renaissance* 37, no. 2 (2007): 215–49.

———. "Spenser's *Faerie Queen*, 6.10.1–4." *Explicator* 66, no. 4 (2008): 237–40.

Secondary Works
"Benjamin Myers—Lapse Americana (an interview)." *The Toronto Quarterly: Literary and Arts Journal.* June 14, 2013. <http://thetorontoquarterly.blogspot.com/2013/06/benjamin-myers-lapse-americana-interview.html#!/2013/06/benjamin-myers-lapse-americana-interview.html>. Accessed: December 12, 2014.
"Myers Receives Oklahoma Book Award for Poetry." Oklahoma Baptist University. http://www.okbu.edu/news/2011-04-14/myers-receives-oklahoma-book-award-for-poetry. Accessed: December 12, 2014.
"Poetry with 'Something at Stake': Benjamin Myers on Past and Present." *World Literature Today* <http://www.worldliteraturetoday.org/poetry-something-stake-benjamin-myers-past-and-present>. Accessed: December 12, 2014.
"Review: *Elegy for Trains* by Benjamin Myers." *Religious Affections Ministries.* October 26, 2010. <http://religiousaffections.org/featured/review_elegy_trains_myers/>. Accessed December 12, 2014.

Selected Poems by Benjamin Myers

Rail Arrives in Rock Island, IL
February 22, 1852

Holding to
the big brown shoulders
of the prairie,
you arrived
to stand firmly at mid-continent,
one long, bony steel finger
pointing west
over the rasping hush of the drying
buffalo grass.

Then,
in a tongue
of steam,
you bent
to whisper softly
to the Irishman,
Go.

Ancestors

Men long and thin like the late afternoon
shadows of the mountain pines,
they followed mules with plows bumping over
rock and red dirt,
listing to one shoulder,
lopsided on the slant of hard Oklahoma hill,

and here
am I
following this lawn mower,
self-propelled
over the easy green.

What would they say to the painless
hush of everyday, the low,
bookish hum of my morning in the office?

I imagine them coming in from the cold
of black and white
photographs, to sit sharply
angled on our leather furniture,
little china coffee cups in blue and white flowers balanced
above the worn places on their trouser knees.

They are silent and looking at me.

I want to explain to them
it is hard where I am
also, the struggle not with rock
nor earth but still to plant
one green thing in minds of my students.

I, too, lie tired and wide-eyed in the darkness.

Road Work

Beneath umbrellas, men with big pink arms
are rolling out the strips of tarred asphalt,
as shiny black as garter snakes and long
as afternoon. The heavy rollers halt,

in dead front of my house, unnerving books
in darkened rooms and worrying china plates,
on cabinet shelves. Gone to the yard, I can
see spots where they, with paint, have marked the grates

and lined the road's new shoulder. Seeing that
my rights of land are safe, I watch the hard
machines climb on the mounds of sweating black
and push the heaps flat near my hapless yard.

The thought that brought me out will teach me to
refuse to draw the far too easy line
between the book and burden of the sun,
that would in fault divide their work from mine.

The men who make the road and man who makes
these words all work the same within our fall.
Those men are builders of a common real,
the makers of the known. And aren't we all?

Land Run

This Land Run Day, I'm inviting
all my Indian friends over for a barbecue.
I'm giving them little plastic tent stakes,
inviting them to claim pieces of my yard.

Our town elders have lined up children
in the park, little girls in prairie-flower
dresses with bonnets tied beneath their chins,
boys in overalls, some with boots: the costume
or imagined costume of their pioneer ancestors.
One girl's father has made a covered wagon
from a lawn-cart by stretching a bed sheet
over five hoops of wire. She pulls
it with a plastic handle.

In the real land run, they came
also by train, the Santa Fe line sagging
down from Kansas so loaded that men
sat on the roof and hung out the windows,
jumping from the slowing train
like fleas from a shaking dog
as it shuddered into Guthrie.

Whole cities were raised in a day: what was
buffalo wallow is now
my backyard drainage problem,
puddle water bulging
with mosquito larvae,
no buffalo shag to soak up
the meager rain.

Bad Harvest

The roving combine crews have moved on north to Kansas,
their hulking green machines wobbling on flatbed trailers.

With little rain comes little wheat, the fields left like a dog
shaved for mange. Mornings, I sit on the porch with the paper

until the heat drives me inside. Last year there was this pretty
cashier at the Dollar General, her face round and nice, but the meth

sucked her inside out bit by bit over the year, so that
by harvest she was old paper from a wasp's nest. I'm thinking

about things that don't turn out right: it's like William Henry
 Harrison,
who won the "common man" with log-cabin-shaped bottles

of hard cider and a reputation in war; science may tell
us his long speech in the rain and cold had nothing

to do with the pneumonia that killed him 30 days
into his term, but what does science know about disappointment?

When I was almost through with college, I crossed a lake
so red you would think only the Pentecostals could have dreamed it,

and lived for a week on the other side, painting my uncle's cabin,
refreshing the white of the trim and railings. Working under

hot glare, I would run into the murky red lake, feet slurping
through leaf rot and mud. Then one day it rained and I sat

on the porch reading Hemingway under clear plastic
sheeting. I was 23 and engaged, dumb as a bull frog,

eating chili from a can and making margaritas
from limeade and cheap tequila. I thought

I was writing a novel. Evenings I would watch the trotline
bobbers nodding into the darkness and each morning

wake beneath mosquito netting on the porch. I actually thought
I was writing a novel. Thank god it didn't turn out that way.

A Letter to Ezra Pound

Ezra, how can I forgive
you?
—the shaking bull
flesh of your throat
rolling hate home from Europe;
did anyone listen?
Ezra, there must have been a pain
hiding like a seed
inside you.

I understand your silence.

Ezra, the moon is low
over the fields tonight;
forget it all.
Come,
the dew hangs
like newborn time
all over the ferns

and peace sleeps lightly on the valley.

An Urgent Message to Li Po

Look, I say, the snow is falling
on our shoulders and hair.
But you say perhaps we
are a thing that is happening
to the snow.

Mysterious God

Armadillo, snake, squirrel:
an archipelago
of carnage down the highway
in August.

The hungry birds
scatter before my hood,
like an interrupted gang
of smoking teenagers:
I'm nearing another
body erupted, a furry
Aetna across both lanes.

Yet, when I arrive,
I find only watermelon rind
flung in broken green and red
on the hot asphalt,
seeds strewn out
almost as if they could grow there.

A Love Supreme

I can't think
of anything
else: that rhythm
like a holy
ghost jungle
cat stalking behind a line
of trees at dusk.

I've got no
right, white
and rural,
to feel about it like this,

but, yes, when
the incense
of that sax
starts twisting
up toward heaven,
my soul,
like a little
brother, comes running behind,
shouting,
"I'm coming too!"
and tripping
on its shoelaces.

Talking to My Racist Friend

I read somewhere that all the sunlight
smacking the earth
at any moment
weighs as much
as a cruise ship,

which makes me
wonder
how much the darkness
in this conversation
with you
must weigh:

Eight semis stacked in a pyramid
and balanced on a teacup?
The Empire State Building
sopping wet?
All the dirt in Oklahoma?

Or maybe a cruise ship
of its own,
with doe-eyed passengers
waving
dumbly from the deck
as they sail obliviously off
to kiss the sullen iceberg.

A Love Poem

There is magic
in the way a woman hums,
sounds as soft as wet summer
nights. Soft as skin.

Remember—
the village women humming
before the storm,
those first shy drops of rain
hiding in their hair,
humming the way
earth will hum like a kettledrum
after the rain.

My grandmother hummed mountains
by revival tents
fluttering like the dove in the breeze
beside the singing river.

Now the woman who calls me hers
hums softly with the wind on the porch swing,
scent of honeysuckle settled behind her eyes.
The same song
swinging softly through the years.
She hums with my head
rested like morning in her lap,
and I know that song.

The Writing Process

The best poems come like freight trains.
The next thought follows from before
until at last nothing remains

on the sky but the graying stains
left by pale smoke on waning clouds, for
the best poems come like freight trains.

One watches the word "Santa Fe"
rolling by on the boxcar door
until at last nothing remains

but to write it before the plains
roll the word to the western shore.
The best poems come with freighted trains

when on the prairie one lone owl sings,
calling darkly to the sick and poor,
until at last nothing remains,

and the hollow-eyed sky brings rains
to wash the dust from the shanty door,
where, like poems, come the last freight trains
until at last nothing remains.

ACKNOWLEDGEMENTS

Cover Photographs

Photograph of Jennie Harris Oliver: Mr. and Mrs. Don Moon Collection, Courtesy of the Oklahoma Historical Society, #11611.

Photograph of Della Iona Cann Young: John Dunning Political Collections, Courtesy of the Oklahoma Historical Society, #23139.G161.

Photograph of Maggie Culver Fry. From "The Lynn Riggs Award." <https://sites.google.com/site/rollielynnriggs/home/lynn-riggs-memorial/the-lynn-riggs-award/2003---maggie-culver-fry>.

Photograph of Carol Hamilton: used with written permission of Carol Hamilton.

Photograph of Betty Shipley: used with written permission of Kathryn Berry, Billy Shipley, and James Shipley.

Photograph of Nathan Brown: Used with written permission of Nathan Brown.

Photograph of Benjamin Myers. Used with written permission of Benjamin Myers.

Photograph of Anne Semple: used with written permission of the *Durant Daily Democrat*.

Poems

Violet McDougal: "The Phantom Round-Up," "The Oil Fire;" "The Knife-Thrower," "University," "Heredity," "The War Drum," "Robert," "The Sharks Jaws," "Greenwich Village Nights," "The Walls of Ossining (Sing-Sing Prison)," and "City Born" copyright © 1925 by The Stratford Company as printed in *Wandering Fires: Poems*. Boston: The Stratford Company, 1925. "Sea Devils" copyright © 1924 by the *San Antonio Express* as printed in *The San Antonio Express*, Dec. 18, 1924, 12. [All in public domain]

Paul Kroeger: "Oklahoma," "Simile," and "To a Fly" copyright © 1935 by Aletha Caldwell Connor as printed in *Anthology of Poetry by Oklahoma Writers*. Ed. Aletha Caldwell Connor. Guthrie, OK: Co-operative, 1935. "The Dance" copyright © 1928 by The Stratford Company as printed in *Contemporary American Poets*. Ed. Horace C. Baker. Boston: Stratford, 1928. "Contrast" copyright © 1925 by *Harlow's Weekly* as printed in *Harlow's (OK) Weekly*, September 26, 1925. [All in public domain]

Jennie Harris Oliver: "Red Earth," "Here," "Noon Trail," "The Desert's Cistern," "Courage," "The Ruined 'Dobe," "Dust," "Hail," "The Feathered Guard," "Orphans," "Lindbergh," "Vingie E. Roe," "Souvenir," "Hackberry Trees" copyright © 1937 by the Burton Publishing Company as printed in *Red Earth: Complete Collection of Poems*. 1934. Kansas City, MO: Burton Publishing Company, 1937. [All in public domain]

Della Iona Cann Young: "October in Oklahoma" and "To the Antelope." No copyright notice provided. Appears as printed in *Old Trails: Commemorating the Old Trails and in Recognition of the Poets Thereof.* Eds. Alberta Guest Clark and Gladys Clifton. Sublette, KS: Press of the *Sublette Monitor*, s.d. [All in public domain]

Anne R. Semple: "These are the Prairie Lands," "Quandary," "Prairie Vastness," "Prairie Lore," "On the Prairies They Say," "The Caddo Hills," "Luminous," "Dancing Thieves," "The Clearing," "The Young Fisher and the Grandpappy Crawdad," and "The Death of Pushmataha" copyright © 1942 by The Kaleidograph Press as printed *Prairie-Born*. Dallas: The Kaleidograph Press, 1942. [All in public domain]

Bess Truitt: "Land Rush," "Symphony," "April Love," "Marriage," "Children," "Talking," "Mid-summer," "A Villanelle," "November," "Maids of Yesterday," "Secrets," and "In Fee" copyright © 1940 by Bess Truitt as printed in *Thistle Down and Prairie Rose*. Kansas City, MO: Burton Publishing Company, 1940. "A Teacher's Plea" copyright © 1963 by *Oklahoma Today* as printed in the Autumn 1963 issue of *Oklahoma Today* magazine. [All in public domain]

Delbert Davis: "My Baby," "The Sandpiper," "Graveyard Gossip," "Flying Saucers," and "Evening at Lake Hiwassie" copyright © 1952 by Delbert Davis as printed in *Pipe Dreams*. Guthrie: OK, Calkins Publishing, 1952. [All in public domain]

Rudolph Nelson Hill: "First Words," "Desert Square Dancers," "On Wolf Creek (A Villanelle)," "Ancient School Appling," "Oklahoma Oil Fields," and "Remembrance in Autumn" copyright © 1965 by Rudolph N. Hill as printed in *Frontiers of Soonerland in Song and Story*. Oklahoma City: Adman Publishing Company, 1965. "Old Santa Fe Trail" copyright ©1962 by Rudolph N. Hill as printed in *Curtain Calls Before Curfew*. s.l.: s.n., 1962. "Bard for Bo-Peep" copyright © 1959 by The Poetry Society of Oklahoma as printed in the *Oklahoma Silver Jubilee Anthology*. s.l.: The Poetry Society of Oklahoma, 1959. "The Oil Fields," "Sonnet of the Plains," and "Fragment of Farewell" copyright © 1929 by Rudolph N. Hill as printed in *Red Ship Wings: Poems*. Wewoka, OK: Lasiter Printing Company, 1929. "Machine Age" copyright © 1954 by Rudolph N. Hill as printed in *Star of Peace on Trail of Cibola*. San Antonio: The Naylor Company, 1954. [All in public domain]

Leslie A. McRill: "Giants," "Logan's Speech," "Burial," "Evil's Snare," and "Messiah" copyright © 1945 by Leslie A. McRill as printed in *Tales of the Night Wind*. Oklahoma City: Dunn Publishing Company, 1945. "Eternal Purpose" copyright 1959 by The Poetry Society of Oklahoma as printed in the *Oklahoma Silver Jubilee Anthology*. s.l.: The Poetry Society of Oklahoma, 1959. "Boomer! Sooner!" and "Sod House" copyright © 1957 by Leslie A. McRill as printed in *Saga of Oklahoma: A Poem of Progress and Growth*. s.l.: Leslie A. McRill, 1957. "Reverie," "In South Vietnam," and "A Rondel" copyright © 1970 by Leslie A. McRill as printed in *Living Heritage: Poems of Social Concern*. Oklahoma City: Leslie A. McRill, 1970. "Old Homestead" copyright © 1972 by Leslie A. McRill as printed in *From Day to Day: As Seen Through My Binoculars*. Oklahoma City: Adman Publishing Company, 1972. [All in public domain]

Maggie Culver Fry: "The Witch Deer," "Cradled," "Indian Ball Game," "Prairie Dearth," "Cherokee Nation, Grantor," and "Green-Corn Festival" copyright © 1955 by Maggie Culver Fry as printed in *The Witch Deer: Poems of the Oklahoma Indians*. 1954. Claremore: Claremore Junior College, 1955. "Willow Wands," "Season in Travail," "The Wheels Keep Turning," "The Featherbed," "Transplanted," and "Eternal" copyright © 1971 by Maggie Culver Fry as printed in *The Umbilical Cord*. Muskogee: Oklahoma Printing Company, 1971. [All in public domain]

Carol Hamilton: "Flatland" copyright © 1991 by Carol Hamilton as printed in *Once the Dust*. Edmond, OK: Broncho Press, 1991. "Face of the War" and "Lambs to Lions" copyright © 2010 by Carol Hamilton as printed in *Umberto Eco Lost His Gun*. Columbus, OH: Pudding House Publications, 2010. "Tealeaves for an Undesignated Reader" copyright © 2011 by Carol Hamilton as printed in *Lexicography*. Greensboro, NC: March Street Press, 2011. "Cain's Ballroom" copyright © 2001 by Carol Hamilton as printed in *Breaking Bread, Breaking Silence*. St John, KS: Chiron Review Press, 2001. "Their Love: The Schumanns" copyright © 2009 by Carol Hamilton as printed in *Contrapuntal*. Georgetown, KY: Finishing Line Press, 2009. "Creation" copyright © 2004 as printed in *The Vanishing Point*. Charlotte, NC: Main Street Rag, 2004. "Pushing Past the Labor Room" copyright © 1994 as printed in *Daring the Wind*. 1984. Edmond, OK: Broncho Press, 1994. "Braced Against the Wind" copyright © 2002 by Carol Hamilton as printed in *Greatest Hits 1968–2000*. Columbus, OH: Pudding House Publications, 2002. [All used by written permission of Carol Hamilton]

Betty Shipley: "Churchyard," "Old Riddles," "Why," and "Because in the Context of Transition Someone in my Poetry Class Asked If I Really Would Like to Meet Jesus—Now" copyright © 1997 by Betty Shipley as

Shawn Holliday is the Associate Dean of Graduate Studies at Northwestern Oklahoma State University (NWOSU), where he directs the new Master of Arts in American Studies program. As Professor of English, he also teaches an upper-level humanities course on the history of rock and roll and various graduate courses in American literature. His books include *Thomas Wolfe and the Politics of Modernism*, a revised version of his Ph.D. dissertation, and *Lawson Fusao Inada*, a critical biography of the former Oregon poet laureate. Holliday's articles and book reviews have appeared in such periodicals as *The Chronicles of Oklahoma*, *The South Carolina Review*, *Appalachian Heritage*, and *The Thomas Wolfe Review* and in such books as *The Encyclopedia of Appalachia* and *Constructing the Literary Self: Intersections of Race and Gender in Twentieth Century Literature*. He also serves on the editorial boards for *Civitas: A Journal of Citizenship Studies*, *The Thomas Wolfe Review*, and *The Researcher: An Interdisciplinary Journal*. A native of West Virginia, Holliday earned his B.A. and M.A. degrees from Marshall University and his Ph.D. from Indiana University of Pennsylvania. In 2009, he and his wife, Susan, moved from Kentucky to Alva, Oklahoma, where they both live and work. As a couple, they are active in animal rescue efforts by feeding and fostering homeless pets, especially ones diagnosed as special needs, and they also volunteer with the Red Cross. After work, Holliday stays active by playing bass guitar with his local blues band Kingfisher and with NWOSU's jazz band. Subsequently, Holliday practices his bass playing at least one hour every day. He has also studied bass methodology with Jack Casady, the bassist for the 1960s rock group Jefferson Airplane and the 1970s blues group Hot Tuna. Already at work on his next book, Holliday is writing a history of Oklahoma literature from the founding of the Oklahoma and Indian Territories through to the twenty-first century.

www.ingramcontent.com/pod-product-compliance
Lightning Source LLC
Chambersburg PA
CBHW020148090426
42734CB00008B/744